The Way to Inner Peace

Buddhism for Daily Living: A Practical Guide

By Kingsley Rajapakse

First edition

Serena Publications, Mississauga, Ontario, Canada

The Way to Inner Peace

Buddhism for Daily Living: A Practical Guide

By Kingsley Rajapakse

Published by:

Serena Publications
Post Office Box 29630
377 Burnhamthorpe Rd. East
Mississauga
Ontario, Canada
L5A 3Y1

Copyright © 1997 by Kingsley Rajapakse
First Printing 1997
Printed in Canada

ISBN 0-9681692-0-1

Preface

The seeds of this book were the essays I regularly contributed to *The Wheel* Newsletter of the Westend Buddhist Center (Mississauga, Canada) over a period of two years. The book would not have been a reality if not for the encouragement I received from many readers, and later, suggestions from the monks at the Center as well as a number of readers, to put together a book based on the essays.

Fundamentals of Buddhism come to us often in heavily laden doctrinal descriptions couched in an unmanageable mix of words of Pali (the original language in which Buddhism was documented) and Sanskrit (ancient literary language of India). Admittedly, doctrinal writings are the essential guideposts that ensure we do not stray from the unchangeable essence of Buddha's teaching. However, to most of us, they do not seem to translate into practical guidelines for daily living.

Buddhism is a way of living that helps to bring out the potential best in us and is intended to be easily accessible to all, not a select few. If we are unable to meaningfully capture the wisdom of Buddhism, as beacons for daily living, then all our preoccupation with dogma and rituals would have served no useful purpose, and we would have missed the primary objective of Buddhism. This book attempts to bridge that gap, to bring into the 'living room' of today's home, the healing essence of Buddha's teaching.

The focus of presentation gradually shifts from an exploration of the key principles of Buddhism needed for effective practice to the actual practice itself. Where appropriate, the 'eye of science' has been used to enhance the presentation. I have tried to make both theory and practice easy to understand, yet not deviate from the primary intentions behind the doctrine or its essence.

The original essays, and now this book, are the products of notes I made for personal use and practical application as I waded through the information maze on Buddhism and other relevant subjects. I hope the reader will benefit from the book at least as much as I did from the notes and thoughts that were generated from what turned out to be, for me, a fascinating exploration.

(Mississauga, Ontario, Canada)   Kingsley Rajapakse

Acknowledgments

For encouraging me to continue with my writings on the theme 'Buddhism for Daily Living', I thank:

- Venerable Bhikkhu Bodhi, President of the Buddhist Publication Society

- Venerable Dhammawasa, Chief Thera, Toronto Westend Buddhist Center and Venerable Muditha, Deputy Chief Thera.

- Venerable Punnaji, former Chief Thera, Toronto Maha Vihara

For reading over and commenting on the final draft I thank:

- Dan Jinapriya, Vivian Macdonald, Janet McLellan and Aloy Perera

For supportive friendship and stimulating Dhamma discussions I express my *metta* to Dan and Aloy.

My very special thanks go to my wife for her patience, understanding and support without which I could not have devoted the major part of my waking hours in the recent past to complete the book.

Contents

1

The Fox and the Mange

No other story from Buddha's life profoundly reveals the cardinal point of his teaching as the following story of the fox and the mange[1].

One day when they were in the forest, the attention of Buddha and his disciples was drawn to a fox that seemed restless. In silence they watched the animal. The fox stood still for a moment. Then it ran under the bush. A moment later it ran out of the bush and stood still again. Then nervously it made a few circles and sat down. Not for long, though. With apparent agitation it ran into a cave. Back again. It jumped up and then ran into the hollow of a large tree. For a while it continued to move from one thing to another. Then, it disappeared out of sight. At that point, the Buddha addressed his disciples thus:

"Monks, you saw that jackal. Standing it suffered. Running it suffered. In the cave it suffered and so did it in the bush. For its suffering it blamed the standing, the sitting, the running, the cave, the bush, the tree hollow and so on. But the problem was not due to any of those. That jackal had mange. That was the root cause. *Until the mange is got rid of, the jackal will continue to suffer ...."*

The Buddha then went on to show that when it comes to the effort to avoid discomfort, the human predicament is the same as that of the fox. We focus on externals hoping to eliminate discomfort and find lasting comfort. But none of that helps, because the root cause of our problem is *wrong views*, or wrong thinking - that is 'our mange'. Until we change our views, we will continue to be unhappy like the fox, no matter what else we do.

Keeping that important revelation from the Buddha in our mind let us travel 2500 years in time and look at our familiar world of today to understand the nature of 'our mange' and how we can get rid of it using Buddhism to create inner peace in our lives. We will do the former in the balance of this chapter and cover the latter in the rest of the book. Let us

---

[1]An itchy skin disease caused by mites.

first take a look at a typical sampling of human existence in today's world.

Little Barny[2] is a bundle of joy as he plays in the park. Equally happy is his mother as she watches him. Later on, when mom says it's time to go home for lunch, Barny protests and continues to play. Eventually a crying Barny follows an angry mother home. One moment joy, another moment unhappiness.

Twenty-five years later, the adult Barny (whom we will now refer to by the unabridged name Barnaby) marries sweetheart Adaline. Life has never before been so joyous for both. Ten years later, they are divorced. He sinks into grieving and she is ever so bitter. One time bliss, then distress.

Blair next door seems happy most often and Barnaby just cannot understand why he is unable to be as happy as Blair, in spite of the effort he puts into life to make it joyous. One person happier than another.

Blair, the only breadwinner of the family, suddenly loses his job of twenty-five years and two years later gets a heart attack. Now Blair feels worse than Barnaby. Reversal of fortune.

Augustina was very attached to grandma. When granny passed away, Augustina was distraught and continued to mourn for weeks. Five years later, while at dinner with the rest of the family, she affectionately recalls funny things granny used to do and they all join in laughter. One time grief, another time laughter.

What we discover is that there is no person who is *totally* happy or totally unhappy all his or her life; happiness alternates with unhappiness. Also it varies from person to person. Undoubtedly, all this variability leaves a common thread of dissatisfaction through human existence. It is this dissatisfaction that creates in us our basic *quest for lasting happiness*, the driving force behind everything that we energetically do in life.

We begin the search as children, intensify it in adult life and continue, in many cases into old age and death, not having found the real thing (lasting happiness), like the experience of most men digging for gems. Why for that long? Because, innumerable times along the journey we feel that we have found it, but then each time to our utter disappointment we find it is

---

[2] All names used are for the purpose of illustration only, with no connection to real persons. In furtherance of that intention, all names have been restricted to those starting with the first two letters of the alphabet - letter 'A' for female names and letter 'B' for male names.

not the real thing, and we move to the next. Each time the experience shows in three clear phases. First, there is the feeling "This is it!" Second, it is tried out. Third, there is the realization, exactly opposite to the first phase, that "This is really *not* it", for it turns out to be either a total disappointment or just transient happiness. So with frustration, the helpless seeker moves onto the next, in an endless quest.

The young child, in one's unconscious search for this elusive entity of lasting happiness, takes refuge in play things. As an older child one may try out things such as a la mode clothing, dyed hair or shaven heads, girl/boy friends and sometimes drugs. The same old story. Not the real thing, so we try the next. Then, as adults our hopes move onto sports cars, university degrees, stock market, marriage, children, the dream home and so on. After all these have been realized, we still find the thing we are most after - unchanging happiness - is missing. "How come," we ask "even after all this time and effort?" Now it is not only frustration, but we begin to get disillusioned with the whole mission of worldly accomplishments. Looking back we realize the nature of the problem all the way from childhood had one common theme: with some things tried out, it has been total disappointment and with the others, transient happiness at most. We find something missing at the very core of being, though the surface may be glittering with acquisitions, with adornments.

On each occasion it is discovered the thing tried out for happiness also causes unhappiness - from the disappointment that Barny experienced to Barnaby's divorce from 'soul-mate' Adaline. And every time each is convinced that someone else's fault caused the suffering. Barny's fun in the park was spoilt because Mom did not bring along a pack of lunch. Barnaby had to go through the trauma of the divorce, all because of the insensitivity of Adaline. Adaline, for her part, is convinced that her life was ruined because Barnaby trapped her into marrying him; else she would have been a happy single woman today and rising up the corporate ladder to ever greater things in that corporation which she quit to get married. Always it is someone else's fault. And so it is with all worldly existence. It is at this point of our desperation that Buddhism comes to our help.

Taking the Barnaby/Adaline example, Buddhism would point out to Barnaby that Adaline is not the *root* cause of his divorce and the ensuing trauma. Whatever Adaline may have done, whatever she may be as a person, all that Barnaby went through emotionally was created by how he perceived Adaline and her actions. Adaline's actions, at most, are to be *associated* with what Barnaby has gone through, but *letting* her actions ruin him happened all within his own mind. To Adaline, Buddhism will bring the same revelation, in principle. So the work both have to do, if they want to eradicate their emotional suffering, is to learn how to change the way they perceive the world, so that they can be in touch with reality; in Buddhist terms, purify the minds. And showing the way to do it is essentially what Buddhism is all about.

As Buddha said[3] "Our present thoughts build our life of tomorrow; our life is the creation of our mind". *Our thoughts come first; feelings and actions follow. Therefore, in order to change the way we feel and act, that is, to alter the direction of our life, we need to change our thinking.* This is the fundamental principle on which the Buddhist doctrine of personal transformation was based by Buddha 2500 years ago and is fully endorsed by science today. We cannot *directly* access our feelings but we can change our thinking so that *indirectly* we have the means to cause our feelings to change. It therefore follows that if we change our thoughts to be in touch with reality, the accompanying feelings are in touch with reality. Now we are one step closer to the solution in our search for lasting happiness.

Five hundred years after Buddha, the Greek philosopher Epictetus conveyed the same deep meaning about thoughts and feelings when he said "It is not the events that cause our feelings but the view that we take of them". Eleanor Roosevelt put it very simply thus: "No one can make you feel inferior *without your consent.*" So all that happens to us, as far as our feelings go, are not caused by the Adalines or Barnabys of this world or other things external to us, but by ourselves in our own minds. That applies not just to our unwholesome emotions, but also to our wholesome emotions (happiness[4] and peace). Hence, while the problem is in our minds, the solution is in our minds too.

Buddhism explains in clear detail very systematically and scientifically the method of moving from unhappiness into ultimate peace - a happiness that is not transient but far surpasses the highest we have ever experienced through sensory contact. That method is the Noble Eightfold Path[5]. For now, instead of venturing into any aspects of the Eightfold Path in detail, let us first try to get a preview of Dhamma practice in a 'nutshell'.

---

[3] From *Dhammapada* 1. Quotations from, and references to, various authoritative Buddhist writings are given throughout the book. The keen student of Buddhism may want to refer to these writings for further study.

[4] Pali term: *Sukkha*

[5] The Noble Eightfold Path is Buddha's way that leads to ultimate peace. The formal list of the eight steps are: 1. Right Understanding, 2. Right Thought, 3. Right Speech, 4. Right Action, 5. Right Livelihood, 6. Right Effort, 7. Right Mindfulness and 8. Right Concentration. In this book we will cover the 8 steps in a manner and practical detail that makes the most meaning for daily living in today's world, rather than strictly follow the classical treatment of the Path. The reader interested in a formal treatment of the subject may refer to "Noble Eightfold Path" Wheel Publication No. 308/311 by Bhikkhu Bodhi. Buddhist Publication Society, 1984.

2

Dhamma In A Nutshell

Not to do any evil, to cultivate good, to purify one's mind - this is the teaching of the Buddhas. *Dhammapada 183*

Buddha showed that there is a way to realize the lasting happiness that we are after and also that we can go beyond what we ordinarily mean by happiness to a point of culmination referred to as ultimate peace[6]. He went onto assure us that the goal can be realized in this very life if we do our part properly. Buddha referred to his universal 'prescription' as Dhamma, meaning teachings (doctrine, laws) pertaining to existence. Dhamma as originally taught by Buddha is essentially a way of wholesome living, with no religious connotations, that guides the practitioner to use his/her mind to its full potential. It is a set of scientific laws applicable to the existence of beings as Newton's laws are for the physical universe. In fact as science advanced, it has been consistently discovering that the fundamentals of Dhamma are in agreement with scientific thought.

After Buddha passed away, outsiders began to call Dhamma by the name 'Buddhism' (meaning teachings of the person called Buddha) and the followers themselves began using the term. With the passage of time, various cultural coatings, rituals, symbolism and the like came to be added to the original Dhamma. These additions arose from a number of reasons such as community needs and sometimes also misunderstanding of Buddha's teachings on the part of some followers. It would be more appropriate to refer to Buddha's teaching as the most scientific psychotherapy ever, rather than religion. Given all these factors, for the

---

[6] The Pali word is *Nibbana* and the better known Sanskrit word is *Nirvana*. This is the highest and ultimate goal of Buddhist aspiration - realized through extinction of craving, aversion and delusion.

purposes of our discussions we will use the term Dhamma whenever we need to refer to the doctrine as originally taught by Buddha.

When Buddha was once asked to explain his teaching in a few simple words, he answered thus: "Cease to do evil; learn to do good; purify your own mind." An assignment simply stated, but a lifetime's undertaking and worth every moment spent in implementing it. As noted earlier, the pinnacle of achievement in Dhamma practice is purification of the mind. However, one needs to create a conducive environment for that mind-purification by good ethical practice. Hence the reason "cease to do evil, learn to do good" precedes "purify your own mind" in Buddha's formula for realizing inner peace.

A closer examination of the message "Cease to do evil; learn to do good; purify your own mind" reveals a further factor essential to the means by which the goal can be realized - that is to focus on the present moment. This becomes clear if we add the implied word *now* to each part of the message. Let us examine each part in that context.

Cease to do evil *now*. This implies no self-blame or guilt (for wrongs one may have done up until now) and no sin (Dhamma knows no sin, only ignorance). The past is to be used, if at all, for growth now, through a knowledge of mistakes made through ignorance.

Learn to do good *now*. Now - the present - is the only opportunity there is to change the direction of one's destiny, stay on the Path and head towards the goal of ultimate peace by wholesome action. This opportunity to do good now also enables us to pay back any dues for any unwholesome deeds done in the past.

Purify your own mind *now*. Again, dwelling in memories of past mental experiences is not going to help a person with spiritual advancement. The prime factor that will determine progress towards peace is what one does *now* to purify one's mind. The means is meditation. This part of Buddha's message also emphasizes purification of one's *own* mind, not another's - the real cure for all problems that exist between people. It comes as a correction to our usual erroneous tendency to blame others.

Having got a glimpse of the building blocks of Dhamma, let us now touch on a few salient points about the journey on the Path itself.

First, *there is no coercion*. While Dhamma promises a path that delivers us from unhappiness into ultimate peace, it does not coerce anyone to follow the Path. It is a try-it-and-see-it-yourself offering. Hence the following admonition from the Buddha[7]:

'Do not go by hearsay; nor upon tradition; nor upon dogma; nor upon the authority of scripture; nor upon reason; nor upon logic; nor upon inference from experience; nor upon acceptance of a mystic experience; nor upon probability; nor upon faith in a teacher. *When you yourselves know*: "These things are good; these things are not blamable, these things are praised by the wise; undertaken and observed, these things lead to benefit and happiness", enter on and abide by them.'

So Buddha himself emphasized complete freedom of thought in one's exploration of Dhamma. What greater encouragement and confidence does one need to explore a promised path to salvation? There is total freedom to enter, walk and if needed quit the path as it pleases the individual. The only thing that keeps one on the path is personal satisfaction with the results of each step already taken. Those who have earnestly entered the Path and did their part properly tell us that the only thing that ever brought them to a halt was the destination.

Second, *Dhamma is for all*. If one were to ask the simple question "Who can benefit from Dhamma?", from our discussion so far we know that the equally simple answer is "Anyone who has a mind". One's religious and other leanings should not stand in the way of straightening out views which are not in touch with reality. Our personal leanings do not come into the question when we try to understand, live with or use Newton's laws of the physical world. The same should hold true for Dhamma, the natural laws that pertain to existence of beings.

Third, we have to *do our own work*. Again Buddha's advice was: "You yourself must make the effort - the Buddhas only point the way." Self-reliance is the key. No different from sensible advice on everything else of significance in our lives. The High School teacher will show you how, but you have to study and pass the exams yourself if you need the High School Certificate.

Fourth, *the work is hard but is achievable*. To change wrong views that have taken root in the deep crevices of the mind over a whole lifetime, and move against further resistance offered by forces unique to the individual (karmic forces) and societal impositions is indeed hard work.

But many have done it and the reward of lasting peace is worth the effort. It requires diligence, dedication and patience from the traveler. Cleaning

---

[7] Source: *Anguttaranikaya*.

one's wound is painful, but once cleaned and the medicine is applied, a pain-free existence follows. The same applies to the journey of liberation.

Finally, *results are verifiable in this very life.* One does not have to wait till heaven or hell, or another life is reached to see 'test results'. The results of 'ceasing to do evil, learning to do good and purifying one's own mind' can be seen right in this life.

In summary, at a practical level what is in Dhamma for us, is a time-tested and well-proven method to help us *permanently* eradicate unhappiness. The method shows us how to achieve this by dealing with the root causes of the problems, namely, wrong views. If the doctor tells you that the root cause of your pain is a potentially cancerous tumor, you would go all out to get the tumor removed. Shouldn't we do the same for our minds? After all, happiness and peace reside in the mind and the greatest therapy in the world is Dhamma.

3

Teachers in Disguise

A man walks down a foot path and encounters an ugly stone. He curses the stone for being in his way and walks on, an angry man. Later, another man, a sculptor with a creative mind, encounters the same stone and promptly recognizes amazing potential in it. Next day, he returns with a wheelbarrow, takes the ugly stone with him, and eventually turns out a prized work of art from it.

In our daily life we encounter many "ugly stones" in the form of problems, mistakes, sickness and so forth, all of which are contributors to some form of *dissatisfaction*[8] (*Dukkha* in Pali), like in the examples we quoted in Chapter 1. We usually look at these as did the first man in our little story above. What we need to do is to change our view to that of the second man, the sculptor and see the amazing potential in the things in our lives that we normally wish were not there. They are all our teachers in disguise. Developing such a view is an integral part of the Buddhist path. Let us now investigate a little deeper and see in what disguised forms our teachers appear.

The first view we have to develop is not only that *dukkha for us worldlings* is a fact of life (the First Noble Truth[9]) but also that it is a *necessity*. Just as much as the ugly stone was necessary for our sculptor to build his prized work of art, we can only realize ultimate peace by

---

[8] Other English terms used are unhappiness, unsatisfactoriness and suffering. The subject is addressed in greater detail in Chapter 6.

[9] Buddha's Dhamma is contained in the Four Noble Truths: (1) There is dukkha, (2) There is the origin of that dukkha, (3) Dukkha can be eradicated and (4) There is a Path that leads to its eradication. The Path is the Noble 8_Fold Path, defined earlier.

working with our "ugly" dukkha. Without dukkha there is nothing on which to work towards Nibbana. From this realization emerge two further insights: firstly, to *accept* dukkha as a part of worldly existence and secondly, to view dukkha as a friend (who helps us progress towards Nibbana), which is a complete turnaround from our usual viewpoint - a transcendental way of thinking. Thus dukkha is our principal teacher in disguise. Given that a major contributor to our stress is aversion to dukkha, such a changed view can become immense therapy, as we begin to accept that embedded in *everything* that happens to us there is the seed of a noble mission. Hence Buddha teaches us within his Four Noble Truths to use dukkha to overcome dukkha - no different to using, in the form of a vaccine, the very virus that causes influenza (flu) to fight influenza.

Those who make our life miserable, particularly those who create the worst times in our lives, are our next group of teachers in disguise. As attempts to change others often end up as futile exercises, the Buddhist way urges us to *look at ourselves*, more precisely to look within, and identify changes needed, using the other person's reaction(s) as our mirror. With that new approach, we will invariably be motivated to take some wholesome action, aimed at changing ourselves, specifically how we view the world around us. That is within our control and will benefit not only ourselves but the other person as well.

The boss one finds impossible to get along with may be the blessing in disguise that causes a person to find another job which is more satisfying. A person who always blames you and never praises, provides you with the wonderful opportunity to practice the art of survival independent of praise and blame and therefore develop the priceless quality of equanimity. ("Even as a rock is not shaken by the wind, the wise man is not shaken by praise or blame" - Dhammapada 81). The rebelliousness of a child may be a hidden message for us to re-examine some erroneous beliefs or values we are trying to impose on the child. The spouse who doesn't do things for you may be the one propelling you on to a path of self-reliance that will one day be your greatest savior. Someone (our "worst enemy") who pushes us to the brink may be just the trigger that catapults us from a life of transient pleasures into the true Dhammic path leading to Nibbana. What better gift can we receive from anyone?

So we must be thankful to those who cause the greatest grief in our lives - we can do this only with a complete shift in our attitude, from the easy and ordinary way of focusing on negativity and blame to one of deep introspection and viewing all that happens as lessons facilitating onward progress.

Moving from disagreeable persons to disagreeable *events*, we can consider the latter as our third category of teachers in our school called Life. Every tragedy has built in it the seed for the germination of a higher purpose, a nobler cause and a gain far surpassing the loss. Numerous are the examples of extraordinary men and women who realized such greater gain over their losses, providing inspiration for the rest of us. Terry Fox, the one-legged runner, raised millions of dollars for cancer research, after his own affliction with cancer. The entire family of Victor Frankl[10], prisoner in World War II Nazi concentration camps, perished in captivity, except for his sister; after release he became one of Europe's leading psychiatrists. Helen Keller, who became blind and deaf at the age of two after an attack of scarlet fever, left a legacy behind, with her contributions to humankind. Such are the capabilities of human beings when they make the determination to transcend their misfortunes. And Buddha demonstrated the pinnacle of such potential when, shaken by the sight of human suffering, he discovered the very remedy - the Dhamma - to transcend all suffering, and made it available to humankind for all time to come.

Our fourth teacher is Nature. We normally speed through life just *encountering* Nature, but seldom *learning* from it. For example, take a fruit tree in our garden. We see leaves at one time, buds later and fruits still later. We pluck the fruits, eat them and we are happy. But the teacher disguised as the tree can teach us the whole of Dhamma, if we care to look more deeply. The birth, decay, old age and death of the leaves and fruits - just the normal processes of Nature, equally applicable to us (and which we usually pretend is not there), is happening in front of our own eyes in just one complete cycle of seasons. Likewise Nature encountered in our daily lives (animals, clouds, our breathing, a feeling of anger, a sick man and so forth) can teach us all the principles of Dhamma, but only if we care to slow down and contemplate. That is mindfulness meditation[11] in action.

Our fifth category of teachers in disguise is our mistakes and failures. We are worldlings because we are not perfect, which is another way of saying we are here to make mistakes until we attain Nibbana. The common way is to blame ourselves for our mistakes and feel guilty, and blame others for their mistakes and get angry. Buddhism trains us to treat our mistakes as our teachers, never to assign blame, take corrective action where

---

[10] Certain aspects of Victor Frankl's story are not too different from those of Patacara, a woman who lived during Buddha's time. She lost her husband, the two children, mother, father and brother in one day. Though she temporarily lost her sanity, Buddha's intervention and a profound exposition by the Enlightened One brought Patacara to the Path and eventual deliverance.

[11] Other terms for Mindfulness Meditation are Insight Meditation and, in Pali, Vipassana Meditation.

possible and accept the things we cannot change. A similar attitude applies to our failures. In reality, there are no mistakes, no failures, no problems but just *happenings* governed by eternal laws of nature. And these happenings provide us with the basis for the next action, with the potential to change our own destiny, if only we choose to use them so.

In summary, if we can train ourselves to always ask the question "What is the lesson this is trying to teach me?" whenever we confront a problem, then with the help of the teacher in disguise we just discovered we will be able to transform our problems (and dukkha) from the 'ugly stones' to 'prized works of art.' Perhaps there is no greater leap we can take on our path to ultimate peace.

4

Living Through Change

(Anicca)

Impermanent, subject to change, are component things. Strive on with mindfulness.

- *Buddha* (Final admonition to disciples)

The one single basic fact on which the whole philosophy of Dhamma hinges is the fact of *impermanence*[1][2].

We all know various changes occur around us but this is often a casual recognition. Rarely do we gain a deeper, insightful, awareness of change as intended in Dhamma, to benefit daily living. It is to realize that deeper awareness that we make impermanence a subject of meditation. Training to gain the *deepest* possible realization of the impermanence of things (first intellectually, then experientially) should be the foremost endeavor of our Dhamma training.

Everything from the tiny atom to the universe itself is constantly undergoing change. In particular, the form of, and the thoughts and feelings within, the human being are constantly changing.

The key to effective living with change lies in developing awareness of the possibility of change *before the change actually takes place*. When we face the actual change, if we were not pre-conditioned to its possibility, then it will lead to more dukkha than it should. We should always be ready for change, rather than let change surprise us - this is one objective of meditation on impermanence. When things are moving well for us, it

---

[12] Two other facts, which *follow* from the fact of impermanence (Pali - *anicca*) are also key to the discussion of Buddhist philosophy. These are dissatisfaction (*dukkha*) and egolessness (*anatta*). These will be addressed in detail in the next two chapters.

pays to remind ourselves once in a while that these will not last forever, then get back to enjoying the good fortune we presently have. Then, when things do change, as they surely will, we can accept the change with equanimity.

All Buddha's teachings eventually contribute to one objective - to help us live our daily lives in such a way that we advance towards the spiritual goal of ultimate peace. Hence, let us see what corollaries result from the fact of impermanence that may help us in daily living - corollaries that we can contemplate once in a while (or during meditation on impermanence) to help ease the burden of change when change does occur.

1. *We normally tend to live as though things do not change.* For example, when we face a difficult situation or a crisis, we often tend to feel the situation will never pass away. But the reality is that, even while we are thinking so, changes are taking place. Given time, the turbulence will settle down to a new situation that is more amenable to problem resolution, or as it often happens, it resolves on its own, just as turbulent water eventually finds its own level of stability. In times like these, one can seek refuge in the profoundly healing message contained in a beautiful story from the East, which has been retold many times with different flavors. The following rendition brings out its essential message:

There was a king whose life was a 'roller-coaster' with regard to everything about him - wealth, kingdoms, family and personal issues. One day a gain, another day a loss. One moment happiness, another moment sadness. The king couldn't continue any more in this fashion, as he was being emotionally drained. He wanted a life of equanimity but did not know how to realize it. So he called his seven sages - the senior advisors. He asked them to come up with the answer by the following day. He told them that he would call them one by one and each advisor who failed to produce a viable solution would be sent to a desolate island.

Next day dawned. The king called the first sage. The solution he proposed was not viable. So he was sent to the island. He called the second - the same outcome. So on it was up to the sixth. Finally, very angry and frustrated, he called the last sage. The sage handed over a ring to the king. The king looked at it and found no relevance to what he was seeking. He became more angry and shouted at his advisor asking him how a ring would solve his problem. To which, the sage responded by respectfully asking the king to read the inscription on the ring. It read "This too will pass." The meaning of the words (that is impermanence of all conditioned phenomena) so deeply penetrated the king's mind, that it immediately imparted a spark of tranquillity he never experienced before. As a result of that deep realization, the king wore the ring for the rest of his life and the inscription always reminded him to view all things and events (the 'good' and the 'bad') with the insight of impermanence. His life rapidly evolved into one of equanimity. In gratitude, he promoted the sage to the highest rank of advisors and arranged for all comforts that could be bestowed on a citizen. The four words "This too will pass" is a jewel for all of us to carry in our minds right through our lives.

Before we conclude this sub-topic, let us also note that we often cling to our attachments as though they will not change and when they do change, the resulting disappointment strikes us down. Again, awareness developed ahead of the occurrence that they will change, will soften the disappointment. It perhaps will help one to completely let go of attachments, which is even better.

2. *No relationship is the same for ever.* The nature of parent-child, employment, marriage or any other relationship changes with the passage of time, due to inevitable change in the parties to the relationship or the surroundings. Insightful awareness of this will help us to tide over change and partings. "Meetings always end in partings".

3. *Our thoughts and feelings change as do physical entities.* Our thoughts and feelings are triggered by phenomena which are subject to the law of impermanence, and therefore are subject to change themselves. Neither good feelings, nor unfavorable feelings are permanent. Often when we are feeling poorly, all that is required is patience (sometimes patience with perseverance) and the feeling passes away on its own. At such times let us again recall the words: "This too will pass".

4. *There is no lasting security in life.* Lasting security implies no change. For example, we wish our health to be as good in the future as it is today. But the incessant and moment-to-moment change taking place within us as well as outside will ensure that we will be subject to illness and decay - so it helps to train ourselves to accept this truth. The only meaningful security that one can have during a lifetime is an inner security that one will deal effectively with every so-called insecurity as it arises, in other words, self-confidence.

5. *Everything in this universe is unique.* Imagine a wave in the ocean as seen in an instant in time. In its make-up, such as composition, movement and shape it is unique. It is unlike any other wave that existed from beginning of time and will be unlike any other that will happen till the end of time. This uniqueness was brought about by moment-to-moment change in all the components of its make-up. The same applies to humans and every identifiable thing in the universe. *Acceptance of the*

uniqueness of all things can lead to profound healing in many aspects of living.

6. *The only reality is the present moment.* Using the same example as before, the wave was reality at the moment it was observed. The next moment, that wave exactly as seen the previous moment is no more reality, but just a memory in the mind of the observer.

7. *Everything in the universe affects everything else in the universe.* Again getting back to our wave, we note that after a few seconds, even the perceptive human eye cannot locate the wave that once was - its components (molecules) have become parts of other waves. After a long time, its components are spread across the world - in waves in the Indian Ocean, in the Atlantic Ocean, in the Great Lakes, may be some in a well, some in a tree and so on.

The fate of the human being is not different from that of the wave. Further, in this case, thoughts, feelings and actions of one human being affect all others within communication reach. Their thoughts, feelings and actions, now influenced to however small a degree, affect others in turn and the cycle continues. The message here, for daily living, is that all we think and do should be wholesome, so that our living contributes to a harmonious world.

Impermanence - we cannot stop it, though it is the primary cause of all our suffering. However, if we insightfully understand it and learn to anticipate and accept it without fear as inevitable reality, then we can harmoniously grow alongside it as we walk on the path towards deliverance.

5

Me and Mine

(Anatta)

Mere suffering exists, no sufferer is found,
The deed is, but no doer of the deed is there.
Nirvana is, but not the man that enters it.
The path is, but no traveler on it is seen.

- *Visuddhi-Magga* [13]*XVI*

The primary factor that differentiates Buddhism from other philosophies of life (including religions) is the fact of no-self or egolessness (*anatta* in Pali) discovered by Buddha and today upheld by science. While the intention here is not an the analysis of all the far-reaching implications of *anatta),* our present objectives would be satisfied if we look at anatta through the eyes of science and also discuss just one early hurdle encountered by most, if not all, who embark on a serious inquiry into the subject. The hurdle is the dilemma wherein we need to, on the one hand, insightfully understand and accept that the self does not exist, while, on the other hand, refer to self constantly in daily life, even after insightfully understanding the concept of no-self.

Let us begin our investigation by reviewing the basic fact of impermanence, particularly as it relates to the human being. The human being is made up of matter (body) and mind. First, let us consider the body. The best way to do this is to look at the cell, which is the basic unit of life. The human body is made up of billions of cells, most of which are so tiny they can be seen only with a powerful microscope. Understanding what goes on inside the tiny cell is one fascinating way to understanding life. Let us do just that.

Within the cells, there is incessant bustling activity, which effectively makes each cell a stand-alone life. The cells absorb substances from

---

[13] Those interested in further study of the subject may want to consult the translation of Visuddhi-Magga from the original Pali into English available as *The Path of Purification* by Bhikkhu Nanamoli (Published by the Buddhist Publication Society, 1991).

outside. They burn fuels derived from food, generating energy, which in turn enables various body functions to be carried out. Then there is waste product elimination. The cells regenerate themselves through division. They synthesize complex substances. Hormones and enzymes, which control vital body functions, are made in the cells. It is the collective (and harmonious) "living together" of the billions of these "little lives" that give rise to what we refer to as the life of the individual. Thus the body is in constant flux.

Next, let us consider the mind, for which the platform of action is the rapid electro-chemical activity taking place in the multi-billion-cell (neuron) network of the brain. The changes taking place in the mind are infinitely faster than in the body. We all know how our thoughts change from one to another to another in never ending rapid succession. Since our emotions are primarily influenced by our thoughts (and to a relatively lesser degree by body conditions such as nutrition), our emotions are also always changing. Further, our memory banks are being constantly updated by new experiences of each additional moment lived. Thus our minds too are in flux.

We can summarize the scientific discussion by saying both mind and body are (and therefore the whole being is) subject to incessant change. Therefore both mind and body are made up of ever changing processes and not fixed entities, although the limitations of our senses create the illusion of pemanency. *Therefore there is no abiding or permanent entity called the self or the ego.* This same observation was made by Buddha 2500 years ago. The difference is that we needed electron microscopes and other high tech support as well as combined efforts of thousands of scientists over many years to come to that conclusion. Buddha, alone, and without the help of even one simple external adjunct, observed the same fact and further extended that to explain the Truth (of life) with his profound philosophy. His extraordinary electron microscope was his fully enlightened, intuitive and deeply penetrating mind. However, it is comforting to know that science today upholds the view of impermanence Buddha held.

Although both science and Dhamma tell us that we should not realistically think of the mind-body combination (that is, the whole human being) as a non-changing entity, yet in daily living we do. We do this primarily by assigning labels such as 'I', 'Me', 'Mine', 'Ben', 'you' and 'Aileen'. Having assigned these arbitrary mental anchors (the labels), we live as though the 'I' is a non-changing entity (that is, self). The only thing that does not change is *the label* 'I' or any other that we created in our minds. Thus we have created an illusion of a non-existent permanent entity (which we, as a species, have got used to calling the 'self' or 'I').

So, when Aileen welcomes her husband Ben after a week away on a business trip, they think they are seeing the same spouse of a week ago. From the discussion on cells, we now know that in reality, it is a different Aileen and a different Ben, in both body and mind. To be precise, we can even go further, and say that Ben who was entering the house is not the same as Ben who is now in the house.

Since the erroneous idea of the permanent abiding self has existed from time immemorial, not only has it become ingrained in the mechanics of human communication but also is *essential* for today's communication; and very likely will continue to be so, as long as the human species exists on this planet. It is no different from saying the "sun rises" and the "sun sets" giving the impression the sun moves in relation to the earth. We know that in reality the sun neither rises nor sets. It is the revolving (movement) of the earth on its own axis that gives us the impression (illusion) it is the sun that moves. Unfortunately, the new understanding (of reality) as to which moves and which doesn't, still will not allow us to now change our ingrained ways of communication amongst fellow beings. We will continue to say "the sun rises", although it is based on illusion. We will continue to say 'heartfelt' when we know the reality is 'mindfelt' - the heart is just a pump whereas it is the mind that feels. Likewise, we will continue to use 'I' and related labels as we have done before.

The most profound healing begins on the day a person insightfully understands this thing called 'self' does not really exist (as a permanent, abiding entity). At the most what we can rightly say is that a self exists only for an *infinitesimal* moment in time, which of course is the same as saying that we are constantly changing - back to impermanence *(anicca)*, the primary law of the universe.

Science helps to understand egolessness (anatta) thus: because, a certain grouping of cells work in harmony, there is a process, for example, that of breathing, but there is *no I* that is doing the breathing - echoing the words of the profound Buddhist quotation we started the chapter with. Breathing is a natural process with no doer, no ownership. Similarly there is the feeling of sadness or happiness, but there is no 'I' that feels. It is essential that one understands this fact without ambiguity, if he or she is to realize the primary benefits that Dhamma has to offer. Once acquired, that understanding will be initially accompanied by a feeling of wastage of an enormous amount of one's past time and effort to protect a self that did not, and does not, really exist. That feeling will soon be replaced by a profound sense of relief as never before felt - a giant step on the path called the 'Dhamma Way'. One's energy flow that was so far used to protect the non-existent self now becomes available in abundance to be channeled to support *noble causes*. Foremost amongst these is to work towards one's own deliverance. Following upon that are endless possibilities such as helping the needy through a sense of compassion and unconditional love for all, spreading the Dhamma and understanding and protecting nature.

A person who has realized the truth of no self will continue to use the 'self labels' to communicate with fellow beings who have not yet come upon that realization, because it is the only way they will understand worldly issues. Even the sentence "There is *no self* in *me*" seems contradictory, but it is not; it is of critical importance that we understand this clearly if we are to make much progress with Dhamma. The only way we can communicate is with sentences like this - we have no choice. Evolution of language has brought us to a point of no return; correcting the incongruity is not possible and we have to continue to live with the problem. Even Buddha, who based his teaching on the fact of no-self, faced the same problem to his last days and used the common terminology of self, as illustrated in this extract from the *Maha Parinibbana Sutta*: "*I* have now grown old and full of years. *My* journey is drawing to a close. *I* have now turned eighty years of age and am now reaching the sum of *My* days. Have *I* not often declared to *you* that it is the nature of things, ..."

Once we have intellectually understood the concept of *anatta*, the mind still needs more work before the concept penetrates the deepest levels of one's psyche and uproots not only the core belief in the self, but also every other belief or behavior which was based on that core belief. This is realized by including contemplation of *anatta* in one's Vipassana meditation practice and also in one's daily living. The following sequence is suggested, with deep contemplation on each listed item as one proceeds through the meditation. (Vipassana meditation is covered in Chapters 13 and 14.)

1. There is no self *(anatta)*.
2. Therefore there is no 'me' or 'mine'.
3. Self, me and mine are terms that only help to communicate.
4. The mind is not mine.
5. The body is not mine.
6. Other living beings, including my family, are not mine.
7. Things are not mine.
8. Therefore there is nothing that is mine.
9. Everything is flux (changing) with no owner.
10. They arise and cease constantly.

Having approached *anatta* from the angle of science, let us now briefly review also one classical rebuttal of the belief in a self. An abiding self, capable of regulating our existence, should be able to ensure that our body and mind do things that we like. For example, if there is this self, and I have some abdominal pain, the self should be able to order and ensure that the pain ceases. Yet we know it cannot be done. Likewise, if a person feels depressed, the self should be able to order its cessation and replace it instantly with a feeling of joy. Again it cannot be done. Examples like these endlessly establish beyond any doubt the non-existence of a self.

Let us conclude this chapter with an analogy. It is 2 a.m. and Brian is having a dream. He sees his dearest brother drowning but cannot help him because Brian does not know how to swim. So in desperation he shouts for help. At that point his wife wakes him and says, "Brian, you had a nightmare. What did you see?"

Now awake, Brian realizes that it was all a dream - an illusion. There was no brother that drowned. There was no dear brother to be rescued.

In real life (to be more precise, 'worldly life' in contrast to 'transcendental life'), when we think of a self (ego), it is like thinking of that dearest brother in Brian's dream. Instead, now it is the 'dearest self.' We worry and 'sweat' through this worldly life thinking there is an all-important self that needs to be protected all the time. Often we think it is in trouble and frantically try to do things, day in and day out, to rescue it. If we can wake up from this long 'dream' of ours (worldly living), as Buddha showed us, we will realize that there is no self to be protected or rescued. Then we will have all life's energy freed to be directed to useful and noble causes.

6

Focus on Dukkha

"Now this, monks, is the Noble Truth about dukkha. Birth is dukkha, sickness is dukkha, death is dukkha, likewise sorrow and grief, woe, lamentation and despair. To be conjoined with things we dislike, to be separated from things we like - that also is dukkha. Not to get what one wants, that also is dukkha. In a word, this body, this fivefold mass which is based on grasping, that is dukkha."

Samyutta Nikaya V

Some of the English words which are closest in meaning to the Pali word *dukkha* are *dissatisfaction*, *suffering* and *unhappiness*. Yet, as we can see from the all-encompassing definition in Samyutta Nikaya, even these English words do not deliver the full meaning that the word dukkha intends to convey. So we will usually use the word *dukkha* in the present discussion and occasionally the English words where context justifies.

The theme of dukkha runs through the whole of Buddha's teaching. After all, it is the First Noble Truth. Accordingly, the reader will encounter through this book direct or indirect reference to this basic fact of existence, as well as means for its eradication based on the teachings of the All Enlightened One. In this chapter, we will review the salient points of the subject, only briefly mentioning those covered in greater detail elsewhere.

A closer examination of the Samyutta Nikaya definition reveals that dukkha falls into two categories - physical and mental. Let us first discuss these in some detail now.

(a) Physical Dukkha

The commonest manifestation of physical dukkha is as *pain* resulting from injury or sickness and also from hunger and thirst. Pain is a physiological mechanism and exists to serve a purpose in beings. That is, to alert the mind to a need for attention somewhere in the body. So pain is something that cannot, and should not, be totally eliminated from the body. Pain can be temporarily relieved with pain killers or Samatha[14] meditation. The other manifestations of physical dukkha are the general deterioration of the body and the pain of death, which may be postponed a

---

14 *Samatha* is meditation aimed at calming the mind. This is discussed in detail in Chapter 12.

little using healthcare, but cannot be eliminated. So there is little we can do to alter the course of physical dukkha.

The important message here is that we need to *learn to accept physical dukkha as an inevitable part of existence* . After such acceptance, in some situations we could proceed to take action to alleviate or postpone the physical dukkha, where such action is possible and desirable. For example, if we have an injury, we can initiate action to have the damage repaired, but we cannot totally prevent the body from being vulnerable to injury in the future.

To the extent that physical dukkha is the disturbance of the status quo, we can if we like, say that physical dukkha is inherent in the inanimate universe too. This depends on the finer meaning we wish to attach to 'physical dukkha'. Viewed thus, physical dukkha merges into the meaning of impermanence itself. Then we can say that physical dukkha (disturbance of the status quo) is inherent in the whole universe.

(b) Mental Dukkha

Most of our dukkha is mental and arises from (a) the way we view objects and events, that is, the external world and (b) the way we view imagined things, that is, all within our internal world. Except for the fully enlightened beings such as the Buddha, we all have mental dukkha, it being a matter of degree and flavor from individual to individual.

First let us discuss in some detail how *the way we view objects and events* brings about our mental dukkha.

The first point we should discuss here is the way we *view* physical dukkha. As noted earlier, if we learn to accept physical dukkha as an inevitable part of our existence, we have just physical dukkha and it stops at that. However, if we superimpose wrong thinking on physical dukkha, then our dukkha is unnecessarily amplified and we suffer more than we have to. This willful addition of mental dukkha to our physical dukkha is a major cause of our suffering.

For example, let's say that Alicia feels a lower back pain. The nature of her suffering can be one of two types depending on the way she reacts:

(1) Alicia accepts the pain as physical dukkha, but knowing that pain is present to alert to something needing attention, she seeks medical intervention. So far she has dealt with her physical dukkha rationally.
(2) Or, the moment Alicia feels the pain, she can jump to a conclusion that it is a slipped disk and imagine many other frightful thoughts

beyond that, such as eventual nerve damage and partial paralysis in the future. Then *she has* superimposed mental dukkha on her actual physical dukkha and she will suffer much more than she really should.

When the medical reports are in, they may reveal the pain was due to a muscular sprain or other minor condition that will heal over a short period of time - that, Alicia will handle objectively. On the other hand, the reports may reveal that in fact it is a slipped disk. At this stage, again her suffering can take the route of one of the two types as before:

(1) If Alicia has trained herself to accept things as they really are (which is the outcome of intensive Vipassana meditation), she will be capable of first accepting a slipped disk as physical dukkha. Then she can proceed to obtain whatever help is available to make the best of the situation. This is easier said than done and very few of us are trained to possess such nonchalant and stoic composure. Yet it's good for us to know the possibilities and Buddhism shows us how to (gradually) develop that mental strength. The dedication and effort one puts in to develop such mental capability, even if not perfected, will bestow significant benefits on the individual. Furthermore, it is prudent to embark on developing such capabilities *before* any eventualities confront us, as mastery takes time.

(2) Or, Alicia can imagine all kinds of horrible things that follow a slipped disk and superimpose immense mental dukkha on the reality of physical dukkha of the slipped disk.

So whether this whole situation will result in only physical dukkha or physical dukkha *and* mental dukkha will be determined by Alicia's mental attitude to things. The good news for all of us worldlings is that our mental attitude is something that we can gradually train to be in harmony with reality, using Vipassana meditation (Chapters 13 and 14).

Besides superimposing mental dukkha on physical dukkha, we humans have a tendency to often do the same over objects and events of the world in general and again cause unnecessary suffering. An example would be how we perceive the hardships of existence a loved one has to go through. Later on we will look at some examples in detail as to how *the way we view objects and events* brings about mental dukkha.

Next let us consider how *the way we view imagined things* causes mental dukkha.

A thought suddenly arising from memory, with absolutely no physical association, can trigger an erroneous thinking pattern and cause us undue suffering. For example, without examining the real likelihood of them happening, we can imagine some such things as a terminal illness or loss of one's residence to fire and trigger further thoughts which will cause undue dukkha. To be secure in the knowledge that if we do face these tragedies (and they are possibilities), we will handle them with equanimity, is the Dhamma way.

Now that we have discussed in general the two types of dukkha - physical and mental - let us review some features of dukkha which may provide us with some insights to ease the burden of having to live with dukkha.

Dukkha is universal - this is perhaps the first thing we need to realize. From the Samyutta Nikaya definition, it is easy to see there are many forms in which dukkha can appear. Though not all of them will comprise the dukkha of any one individual at a given time, dukkha is part of living for all of us *worldly* beings, just as breathing is. It is only when we have transcended worldly living that we would have transcended dukkha. Birth, sickness and death form a common denominator for all beings. So, while we are youthful and healthy, we may encounter few of the manifestations of dukkha, but it is a matter of time before other forms confront us. In spite of all our technological and other advances, the fundamental dukkha that confronts us remains the same as it has always been, including in Buddha's lifetime.

While one could easily accept sickness and death as dukkha, the question may be asked why birth is dukkha - after all, we are used to associating childhood with joy and happiness. The answer becomes abundantly clear if we look at these undeniable *facts*. (1) A child enters this world with a cry of pain at birth. (2) All other dukkha happens because one is born - if there is no birth, there is no dukkha. (3) Childhood is not all happiness but a mix of happiness and unhappiness. A child plays at the park and giggles with joy; the child also falls down, bruises himself/herself and cries. Children become sick as do adults. However, all things considered, we can say that there is usually less mental dukkha in childhood than during other stages of life. (4) Childhood is impermanent - it becomes only a matter of time before the child moves into youth, old age and death with the attendant dukkha.

Buddhism (Dhamma) is based on hard truth and often truth causes initial discomfort in us because we are used to living in a world of relative truth or illusion. If we want to transcend suffering, even with mental discomfort we should be prepared to face the truth. Then, with time the discomfort gives way to a level of comfort and peace (based on solid reality) that we have not experienced before.

Therapy for dukkha is to train ourselves to acknowledge its existence but not own it. This becomes obvious when we recall and deeply contemplate on (1) the fact of no-self (anatta) and (2) the profound words of Visuddhi-Magga quoted earlier "Mere suffering exists, no sufferer is found ....."

Happiness always carries latent *dissatisfaction.* Due to the operation of the primary law of impermanence, with time what is now satisfactory will change to a state of dissatisfaction, either as direct manifestations now or as latency to surface later. So there is always latent dissatisfaction in worldly living. For example, I could be having an adorable pet dog now and enjoying its company. However, for sure it is a matter of time before the dog and I have to part company and then the present satisfactoriness changes to dissatisfaction.

Impermanence exists regardless of a perceiver. Impermanence viewed by a perceiver in a certain manner becomes mental dukkha Though every object or event in this universe is a manifestation of the primal cosmic law of impermanence, it inherently does not contain an element of mental dukkha. Impermanence is a neutral phenomenon in the universe at large. It is only when a perceiving agent interprets any manifestation of impermanence through ingrained views which are not in touch with reality (wrong views) that it turns into mental dukkha and that is, in the mind of the perceiver. It is like clear water in a lake which is neutral in color. However, if we look at the water through colored eyeglasses, the water too appears colored. So, to emphasize, any manifestation of impermanence needs two conditions, (a) a perceiving agent and (b) wrong views through which the perceiver sees the manifestation, for it to be perceived as mental dukkha.

In a way, we can say that we perceivers 'intrude' into manifestations of impermanence with our senses and thereafter view that manifestation with wrong views, thereby causing mental dukkha for ourselves. That is, sensory intrusions, combined with wrong thinking, cause mental dukkha. For example, I *see* rain (intrusion with my sight), then think "What a lousy day it is" and I feel depressed (mental dukkha). Or, I *hear* the neighbor's dog bark (intrusion with my hearing), wish it didn't bark (wrong, futile thinking) and get angry (mental dukkha). So the way out would be to avoid sensory contact (which is not always possible) or change the way we view the manifestation to one that is in touch with reality (replace ignorance with wisdom). The latter always works, though it takes time to penetrate our lives. Thus, in our examples, we can learn to accept both rain and the barking of the dog as just the way things are at the moment and thereby alleviate the mental dukkha. The important message here is this: *if we train our mind to enable us to live in harmony with the world, i.e., 'go with the flow of nature', then we are at peace.* In contrast, if the mind's reactions result in disharmonious living, then we continue to suffer.

Our accustomed way is not to see impermanence (change) as such, but to interpret it as mental dukkha. This is primarily caused by the underlying wish in us for things that we like to remain as they are - the ego, our youth, good health, dear ones and so on. To that extent mental dukkha is inherent in *human* existence, caused purely by how we perceive things. Hence Buddhism lists dukkha as one of the basic facts of existence - that is, *worldly* existence. Buddha's teaching shows us the transcendental way, that is to see impermanence as impermanence, hence transcend mental dukkha and realize peace. Thus, from whatever aspect of Buddhism we approach, we encounter the recurring emphasis to change our erroneous views (see things as they really are) in order to eradicate dukkha. Once we accept impermanence as impermanence and do not add our own coloring to it in interpreting, we have wisdom instead of ignorance and we are on our way to peace here and beyond. This point being of critical importance to our healing, let us look at a few examples, to help us solidify this principle in our minds.

In countries that experience the four seasons, generally people are happy when they see signs of Spring and are overjoyed when Summer arrives. With the onset of the Fall, their moods wane and finally when winter arrives they are sad.

Now imagine that due to some cause, we the perceivers suddenly cease to exist on the planet. Will the seasonal changes - Spring to Summer to Fall to Winter - continue to happen? Of course - year after year. And that occurrence is caused by impermanence - the fact that the sun and the planets don't stay in one place but are subject to constant change of position. Impermanence exists and continues to exist stubbornly and aloof, as a cosmic principle, whether we perceivers are there or not to interpret it as dukkha. Thus, to be precise, 'suffering' (or 'dukkha') is a concept only in thinking beings.

So if we deeply accept the fact that the change of seasons (particularly onset of Fall and Winter) is exactly the way it is supposed to be, and not wish it to be otherwise, then we would have transcended our worldly (erroneous) way of thinking, transcended dukkha on this issue and would be on our way to better moods and contentment in winter time.

As the next example, consider the death of a loved one. This is something that we all have to face sometime or other in our lives. This, like the change of seasons, is a fact of nature dictated by impermanence and there is nothing we can do about it - what is born has to die. This natural event, when it happens, is usually transformed into one of much dukkha, in the minds of those still living. This is due to ignorance, specifically non-acceptance of impermanence of human existence. However, if we include the subject of impermanence in our daily meditation, and practice it over a reasonable period of time, our minds can be conditioned to help us cope with such situations with much less dukkha when the inevitable events do confront us.

As the third example, take the case of our feelings in general. Feelings shuttle between pleasant and unpleasant from time to time within a day and from day to day. This is due to changes taking place in (a) objects and events in the world around us, (b) the operation of our sensory mechanisms, (c) neuro-chemical activity in our brains and (d) our perceptions. We create dukkha when we wish our pleasant feelings to stay (clinging) and the unpleasant feelings to vanish (aversion). However, if we train ourselves to accept that both pleasant and unpleasant feelings are caused by impermanence and that whatever feeling we have now will not stay the same for long, we would have alleviated a lot of dukkha in our lives.

With the focus on dukkha, Buddhist teaching starts with a realistic view of human existence. A common question that Buddhists are asked is: Since Dhamma refers to dukkha often, doesn't it teach a pessimistic world view? A simple and straight answer can be put in two parts: (a) Buddhist teaching is neither pessimistic nor optimistic but realistic - it pivots on truth and truth only and (b) while Dhamma starts off describing dukkha (because that is the fact of life), its lasting gift to humankind is a method (the Noble Eightfold Path) for the *eradication* of dukkha. In Buddha's own words: "Not only the fact of dukkha do I teach, but also the deliverance." (Anguttara-Nikaya). It is no different to a doctor first telling a patient that he has a viral infection, and then, that he will prescribe the medicine to cure it. It was not pessimism on the doctor's part to first tell the patient about his problem. Likewise, Buddha has effectively told us all "You have dukkha. I will give you a prescription to cure it." There is absolutely no pessimism in that disclosure of truth and cure.

As a simple example to illustrate the above, take the case of aging. The usual worldly approach is to view aging with negativity - with pessimism. As opposed to that, some current 'optimistic' approaches are based on training adults to enact some desirable aspect of childhood which was missed in real childhood. This approach, although it may produce some transient mental benefits, is bound to fail sometime because as a person gets older the imaginary re-creation of aspects of childhood become more and more impractical and finally impossible, creating a worsening dilemma with the passage of time. The realistic approach of Buddhism views both birth and old age, as well as all stages in-between, as *equal* concomitants of the cycle of existence laden with dukkha and further proceeds to show how the dukkha can be eradicated. The focus is dukkha and its eradication and not age or age groups. Thus old age is neither superior, nor inferior, to birth and childhood and vice versa. That is a stable and solid view for people in all phases of life to take because it is based on absolute truth, instead of trying to mentally (and artificially) re-create a phase of life that is past and gone forever.

The root cause of dukkha is wrong views (erroneous thinking). Thinking (wrongly) is mental dukkha. Hence, meditation, which is the core of Buddhist teaching is directed at changing one's thinking from the accustomed, conditioned and erroneous ways to one of transcendental thinking ('seeing things as they really are'). Samatha meditation calms the mind by helping it to focus on a simple object such as one's breath and thereby bringing thinking to a virtual *stop* during meditation. Once a person has mastered a reasonable degree of skill and confidence in Samatha, one can proceed to Vipassana meditation, where the (now-tamed) mind is willfully directed to see things as they really are, thus eradicating mental dukkha created by the earlier distorted perception. The primary facts one is trained to realize in Vipassana are impermanence (anicca) and no-self (anatta). 'Seeing things as they really are' does not mean just acceptance of things as they really are. Rather it implies, first an acceptance, followed by necessary action in the present moment to change the direction of one's existence to one of wholesomeness. More on meditation in chapters 12, 13 and 14.

Dukkha is our principal teacher. When we contemplate the truth of worldly existence, which is dukkha, we are able to develop wisdom and transcend that very dukkha. Therefore dukkha is our principal teacher in disguise. Rather than developing aversion to dukkha, or wanting to run away from it, we need to learn to work with it. Suffering is an opportunity for profound spiritual growth. If we have extraordinary suffering, we have an extraordinary opportunity to accomplish an equally extraordinary mission, speeding up our enlightenment process. We need, however, insight to perceive the opportunity that is clothed to appear as dukkha - that is to see dukkha as a teacher in disguise.

7

Our Sensory World

Who is free from sense perceptions
In him no more bonds exist;
Who by insight freedom gains
All delusions cease in him;

But who clings to sense perceptions
And to viewpoints wrong and false
He lives wrangling in this world.

Sutta Nipata, Verse 847

Let us imagine for a moment, that all our senses (sight, hearing etc.)
are disabled. Then, the world perceived by us immediately ceases to
exist, even if all our other organs (such as the heart) and functions (such
as blood circulation) are intact. Thus, the very foundations of our
perceived existence - the 'world out there' and 'me witnessing that world'
- are made possible by our senses, though, collectively the sensory
mechanisms comprise a very small proportion of the human body. In
fact, the most profound and significant teaching of the Buddha - that of
Dependent Origination[15] - is formulated on our sensory system and not
the rest of the body. Hence, to obtain a meaningful insight into
Dhamma, we need to equip ourselves with at least a minimal
understanding of our senses.

There are six senses in all. Of these, five are easily evident to us - they
are sight, hearing, taste, smell and touch. Before we try to identify the
sixth, let us take one of the five senses and get a glimpse into the
sensory process by walking through the important events of that
process from beginning to end. We will take the sense of sight for our
illustration.First let us try to understand the mechanics that help us see
things. Consider light falling on a certain object ahead of us. The light
rays that are reflected from this object enter our eyes and form an image
on the retina. Then electrical (nerve) impulses carry information about
the image from the retina to the part of the brain dedicated to the

---

[15] *Paticcasamuppada* in Pali

function of sight. From information received about this specific image, and by matching this information against existing data, the central processing part of the mind makes a series of quick associations at 'lightening' speed, invariably aided by additional visual interactions with the object to gather supplementary information. All this happens with great rapidity.

We will now get an idea of the process of associations and their sequence, by looking at what is happening, in 'slow motion', or rather, as converted to the equivalent of a 'slide show'. Note that in real life the perceiver (we will call him Bertram) is unaware of the individual 'slides' because of the immense speed - he sees only the 'movie' and not the 'slide show'.

The first association is objective and close to reality - simply of form, movement and color and corresponds to what is referred to as the 'bare object' in meditation - the unadulterated view. As we progress from this point on, the mental associations become more and more subjective (and judgmental). The events in the sequence are many; we will select only a few that are important for our discussion. In our present example, these associations (as perceived by Bertram) may be somewhat like:

1. It is an object, white, moving.
2. It is a man.
3. It is Cousin Burl.
4. Cousin Burl is the selfish, mean and obnoxious person, who has never spoken a good word to me.
5. I always end up in a confrontation with him.
6. I hate Cousin Burl

Thus it is easy to see how something that started as a simple sensory trigger (in this case sight, of a moving form) eventually leads to the subjective reaction of hatred or aversion as it passes through, and is evaluated against, layers of existing data in Bertram's mind. In another case[16], the sequence of the 'slide show' as 'seen' by Bertram may be: (1) It is food, (2) The food is peach ice-cream, (3) peach ice-cream is delicious and (4) I want to eat peach ice-cream (although I just finished eating the dessert of pudding!). Here Bertram ends up with craving.

The same kind of processing applies to the other senses - hearing, smell, taste and touch. In fact, each and every one of the innumerable

---

[16] We will use the same examples to illustrate and clarify a number of other points as we progress through the book.

sensory interactions we experience in a day passes through this process resulting in either aversion or craving. The key points to note are (a) the five sensory contacts bring information about the world around us into our brain (we could use the term 'mind' in place of 'brain' as the process moves into the subjective phase), (b) the mind processes that information, (c) it compares this information to existing data, i.e., views, concepts, images etc. already rooted in the mind (from previous experiences), (d) the mind makes judgments/conclusions about the object or event and (e) craving or aversion follows, and hence feelings. In passing, it is important at this point to recall (from Chapter 1) that first comes our thinking and *then* our feelings, of either dukkha (dissatisfaction) or sukkha (happiness).

Now what is the sixth sense? It is part of the mind itself - to be more precise, the mind's storage area, that feeds a triggering thought to its information processing area. The triggering thought in this case becomes the 'sensory' input, although it is not from a true sensory mechanism with physical parts and, more importantly, this sense does not interact with the external world. If you like, you may think of it as connecting to an 'internal' world, which is all within the mind. Let us consider an example to clarify and illustrate the sixth sense again with Bertram as the perceiver.

He is seated at the beach with his eyes closed. Suddenly a picture or thought of the peach ice-cream arises in his mind - this is the 'sensory' trigger. Once the trigger is made, the processing is identical to the earlier example (where peach ice-cream was actually sighted), ending in craving. Likewise, a triggering thought about Cousin Burl may suddenly arise in Bertram's mind and as before he ends up with aversion, although this time Cousin Burl may be miles away. Thus, for craving or aversion to occur, we do not necessarily have to receive input from the world outside through the five senses that have physical appearances, but they could all be generated from within the mind itself - simply through imagination. In fact, if we look at all six senses together, the most important sense is the sixth - mental image. This is because we happen to cause more dukkha in ourselves through imaginations, than through the senses of sight, sound, taste, smell and touch.

We know the mind is often unable to cope with the incessant overloading of information to it by the six senses, often in competition, all seeking priority attention. When a person is really unable to cope with this overload, then it results in confusion. The six senses may be compared to six hyperactive tentacles of an octopus, all of which, in competition, are endlessly bringing in their collections to the octopus's body. Another analogy would be six rambunctious children who are driving a mother crazy. Buddha compared this problem created collectively by the six senses to a cow skinned alive. Flies settle on the bare body irritating (confusing) the animal endlessly, just as the information arriving via the six senses confuses the mind. The solution to the problem? Meditation.

Our eyes are designed to see continuity as permanency (the 'movie') and not impermanence (the 'slide show'). We see a tree today and tomorrow we see the same tree, because our eyes cannot see the incessant cellular activity (change) that is taking place inside that tree. So the tree *appears* to us as a solid entity. The same applies to our other senses. This apparent continuity is then another reason for our erroneous belief in an abiding self when there is no such thing.

Our senses are extremely limited in what they can do - for example, human hearing and vision take up a very small (almost negligible) part of the total frequency spectrum [17]. The rest can be 'sensed' and used only by instruments and machinery that belong in such technologies as radio, TV, microwave and X-rays. Nature has designed (and evolved) our senses for survival and not for us to see reality. Nature does not care whether we see reality or not, or for that matter, whether we suffer or not. So we have to consciously transcend our senses to see reality. Hence the need for meditation, which is a technique invented by human beings to get around the inherent handicap of restricted senses that prevent us from perceiving reality.

The inherent limitations of our senses also should caution us to be very careful when we try to impose on others our sensory observations as the truth or reality. There is a lot going on in the universe that our senses cannot perceive. What we can know of this universe with our senses is negligible, a mere 'drop in the ocean' compared to what lies outside their grasp. We cannot discard possibilities outside our sensory detection as untrue. Of what we do not have the power to know, it would be only prudent and realistic to say "maybe" and leave it at that.

Earlier we saw how the six senses lead to craving or aversion. But why is craving or aversion the major existential 'sin'? For the answer let us look at an analogy.

Step outdoors in the night and watch the activity around an intense light or flame. Insects like moths and beetles head towards the source of light

---

[17] The frequency spectrum is zero to 10^{22} hertz which is an enormous span by any standards

only to meet with suffering - to be roasted to death. Why do they move towards their destroyer? Because the sensory interaction with the flame brings about a feeling of pleasure. The transient pleasure gives rise to craving, the insect is attracted to the object and it moves to its destruction. Thus, the transient pleasure is an illusion of permanent pleasure, a bait which succeeds in deceiving the insect.

The human predicament is identical to that of the insect, except for one very important difference. We humans are equipped with the power to think (to develop *wisdom*), if we care to use that capability, whereas that insect, lacking that capability, remains in *ignorance* and is doomed to move towards its own destruction. From the viewpoint of the paradox of basic existence, we are just 'moths given the ability to think' and therefore to realize the consequences of our actions. Unfortunately, it is a fact of humanity that we, in this worldly existence, let craving and aversion guide the course of our lives, fooled by the bait of transient pleasure and, like the ignorant moth, move towards our own demise, which awaits us at the end of that transient happiness.

Therefore, moving from ignorance to wisdom becomes our savior, and follows from link number one of Dependent Origination. While a complete description of Dependent Origination and a thorough examination of its implications are obviously much beyond the scope of this book[18], we will restrict ourselves to drawing out a formula from it to show us, in simple and practical terms, how we may apply it to resolve our day-to-day problems.

The doctrine of Dependent Origination explains the ramifications of existence of beings, the suffering within that existence and how to bring about a cessation to that suffering. It is based on the universal and scientific principle of cause and effect[19]. Its pivotal building block is a chain of twelve cause-effect links and is usually explained in terms of three consecutive lifetimes. However, a selection of the links can be used to explain every *individual event* that takes place within one lifetime - most importantly, this life of ours. We will restrict our present investigation to the latter.

Now to determine how we can apply this doctrine to daily living, we need not be concerned here with all the twelve links - some of them are

---

[18]Those interested in a deeper study of this doctrine are invited to consult "The Great Discourse on Causation. The *Mahanidana Sutta and Its Commentaries*" translated from the Pali by Bhikkhu Bodhi and published by the Buddhist Publication Society, 1983.

[19] The principle of cause and effect is discussed in detail in the next chapter, under the title 'Tolerance and Action'.

primarily of theoretical interest. Thus, just as we can ignore the wiring and say the operation of a switch causes a light bulb to light, we can extract the practical portion of Dependent Origination:

(1) **Ignorance** causes Reaction to occur
(2) **Reaction** causes Sensory Contact to occur
(3) **Sensory Contact** causes Craving* to occur
(4) **Craving** causes Clinging (attachment) to occur
(5) **Clinging (Attachment)** causes *suffering* to occur

   (*   Note that aversion too is usually considered a *craving* - craving for the non-existence of something)

This simplified formula of Dependent Origination reveals two important insights into what we can do to eradicate dukkha:

(a) Eradication of Ignorance causes all the other links to cease and therefore eradicates dukkha permanently. As we know, this takes time.

(b) Since ignorance is the root cause, even if we can sever any of the links 2 to 5, dukkha will be curtailed only temporarily. This is because ignorance will recreate links 2 to 5 (just as a tree pruned to the level of trunk and roots will eventually cause branches and leaves to reappear). Yet, this capability to willfully avoid or curtail our reactions, sensory contacts, craving and clinging gives us a *temporary* way out from dukkha, while we are working to eradicate the root cause, that is, deep-rooted ignorance.

Our whole life is an enormous collection of individual events. Therefore, eradication of suffering from our life is made up of eradication of suffering on each individual event lived through and experienced from moment to moment. Thus, Bertram's encounter with Cousin Burl was one of those events in Bertram's life and suffering arose within Bertram due to the anger, anxiety and tension he created within himself by the way he thought about, and perceived, Cousin Burl. So getting help from Dependent Origination as discussed above, the following is the kind of action that is available to Bertram:

- For temporary relief he can: (1) *not react* to Burl's ways, for example, not talk back when Burl is obnoxious towards Bertram, (2) go for a walk when Burl visits (*avoiding sensory contact of hearing and sight*), (3) go into a quiet place and do some breathing meditation (*avoiding 'sensory contact' of mental triggers*) and (4) remind himself that aversion is an unwholesome action.

- For permanent relief Bertram has to see which deep-rooted views caused him to dislike Cousin Burl. Buddhist teaching shows clearly the very fact he had an aversion towards Cousin Burl (and suffered), indicates he harbors a set of basic wrong views that caused his averse perception of Burl. We will pursue this aspect further in Chapters 13 and 14.

Dependent Origination applies to any and all of our life situations as in this simple example - it explains the problems and provides the solutions. As we can see, the replacement of basic wrong views with the corresponding right views becomes an important part of Dhamma practice. Specifics of how this is done, and what are wrong views and their corresponding right views, are provided in later chapters. For now, suffice it to say it is achieved through a *deep understanding*:

1. Of impermanence and egolessness and important corollaries that follow from them, solidified with the help of the practice of *Vipassana* (Insight) meditation.

2. That (a) our reaction to situations, objects and events leads to craving/aversion and (b) that craving/version leads to our destruction, as it did for the moth.

Replacing wrong views with the corresponding right views in this one event is an example of moving from ignorance to wisdom on that *one event*. If we do likewise for all other events in our lives (the task becoming easier as our practice gathers momentum), then it becomes a *life* of wisdom - hence the vehicle to permanent peace.

8

Tolerance and Action

(Karma)

"Undisturbed shall our mind remain, no evil words shall escape our lips; friendly and full of sympathy shall we remain, with heart full of love, and free from any hidden malice; and that person shall we penetrate with loving thoughts, wide, deep, boundless, freed from anger and hatred"

- Buddha (From the Majjhima-Nikaya, No. 21)

"When a man has something to do, let him do it with all his might."

-Buddha (From Dhammapada 313)

The doctrine of *karma* is one of the cornerstones of Buddhist teaching and its understanding is therefore essential to the proper practice of Dhamma. *Karma* in Sanskrit (and *kamma* in Pali) means 'action' or volitional deed. The most important aspect of action, within the context of karma, is its ability to produce results that correspond to the moral nature of the deed. Thus karma is a doctrine of moral retribution. Due to the inherent difficulty in understanding ramifications of moral retribution, karma and its results applicable to beings are sometimes compared to cause and effect applicable to the physical universe, a concept that we can relate to easier. For the purpose of our discussion, we will follow that route, equating action to cause and result to effect.

Cause and effect is a fundamental law of nature. If I do not eat healthy food and exercise (cause), then my immune system weakens and I fall sick (effect). Strictly speaking, what is usually at work is the collective action of multiple causes rather than a single cause and it is best to clarify this point first.

When we investigate accurately to determine what caused an event, we find one outstanding cause and a number of relatively less apparent 'supplementary causes' (conditions) at play that collectively brought about the event.

To illustrate, let us take the case of a seed and plant. We would usually be quick to say that the seed is the cause of the plant. But there are many conditions such as correct temperature, soil composition, moisture content and sunlight, the absence of any one of which will prevent the plant from being formed and nurtured. We may call all of these factors - the seed, the correct temperature, soil composition, moisture content and sunlight - 'conditions' or 'causes'. Alternatively, we may call the seed (the outstanding factor) the 'cause' and the other factors 'conditions' - this seems to be the common usage. It really does not matter much because these are mere terms (concepts) used to communicate. What is important is that we should not lose sight of the principle that phenomena (things and events) arise because of prior conditions (or causes). This principle is usually referred to as conditionality or causality. This is also the pivotal principle on which Buddha's profound doctrine of Dependent Origination[20] is based.

Besides the fact that things happen due to multiple causes, another important conclusion of this principle is that there is no '*first* cause' for anything. Thus the plant we referred to above came into being because of a set of immediately preceding conditions. Now if we take just one of those conditions, say the seed, we know that it came into being because of prior conditions which include its parent tree. This chain extends backwards endlessly in time creating a maze of unfathomable complexity.

One important lesson that we can learn from this discussion on causality is that when it comes to dislikeable events in our lives, it would be erroneous for us to blame immediate apparent causes (such as a blunder made by a family member) as *the* cause of what happened - it is one of a myriad causes, though it may happen to be the closest to the event.

Now let us return to our discussion on karma. Divide karma into past and present and the essence of Buddhist teaching on karma shines through, as the sunlight beams through the parting clouds.

---

[20] Dependent Origination (*Paticcasamuppada*) was discussed earlier in Chapter 7: Our Sensory World.

Past karma, applied to human life, is the cause-effect chain up to this present moment. The facts about past karma are:

- It cannot be changed.
- It contributes to making each one of us (6 billion human beings) unique, and also each moment within one individual's life unique compared to every other moment of his or her life, as one progresses through one's karmic path.

What the above two facts clearly tell us is that, if our lives are at all to be rational and sane, we must totally and gracefully accept what has happened, that is, we must show *tolerance* towards what is. This is why Dhamma emphasizes "acceptance of the way things are" as an integral part of its teaching. This means we accept ourselves, other human beings and all of nature without judgment and without wishing that things should be different. It also means we do not blame any person or nature for what has been. Here, to quote the Dhammapada (#50): " Let none find fault with others; let none see the omissions and commissions of others. But let one see one's own acts, done and undone".

Tolerance is not a quality that can be developed directly but is a by-product of deep understanding of, firstly, the uniqueness of all living beings and all things that make up this universe and, secondly, their right to that uniqueness. The understanding leads to acceptance and acceptance to tolerance. Thus, the practical means to acquiring the quality of tolerance is to insightfully understand the uniqueness of ourselves and everything else in the world around us.

As did many other great thinkers and teachers, the Stoic Philosopher Epictetus echoed in summary (five hundred years after Buddha) Buddha's emphasis on the need for acceptance with these profound words: "True instruction is this: *To learn to wish that everything should come to pass exactly as it does*". Buddha's advice on acceptance and tolerance surfaces in many of his teachings and nothing could be more appropriate for re-alignment of relationships - personal, social and regional - in today's world.

So far we have examined past karma and how it inevitably leads to a need for tolerance in daily living. Having shown tolerance towards what is, do we stop at that? Absolutely not. This is where the second part of karma - *present karma* - comes in. Present karma gives us the opportunity for willful **action**. Although we cannot change what has happened (past karma), and it determines our present, *we can influence our future by choosing our present action*. Thus our complete code for living is not passive acceptance of the way things are, but *acceptance followed by meaningful action.*

The inter-relationship of the triad - past karma, present karma and willed action - can be compared to that of the wheels of a front-wheel-drive car. The rear and front wheels together provide for the movement of the car. Yet change of direction is possible only with the front wheels, because the steering wheel is connected to the front wheels. The rear wheels are past karma, the front wheels the present karma and the steering wheel the will.

Action entails determining what we can do about the situation we have accepted as reality, to make life better and to do it forthwith. And one needs to accept gracefully what is not within one's capability to change. And here one is reminded of words from the Christian prayer "..... the serenity to accept the things I cannot change, the courage to change the things I can and the wisdom to know the difference".

We generally know the virtues of tolerance but usually find it difficult to practise it in daily living. Someone does something we do not like and we get upset and may even translate our feelings into verbal or physical expressions. An event occurs that brings us difficulties or discomfort (such as a snowstorm or job loss) and we may grumble, get angry or depressed. Such reactions are counter-productive and negatively affect not only our long-term health through stress but also the world we interact with, our relationships, and most importantly, our spiritual growth. The antidote is tolerance (acquired through understanding) followed by appropriate action.

We have so far seen how past and present karma translate into tolerance and action in daily living, in principle. Now let us see, with examples, how these principles actually apply to individual life, inter-personal relationships and nature.

If I had an altercation with my friend, and now I realize I had been unfair, I should first show tolerance and understanding to myself - no blame, no guilt, just compassionately understanding that I was at a unique karmic moment on my life's path (tolerance - of oneself). I phone my friend and say "sorry" (action). I also resolve to use this experience to act differently in the future (further action). The same should apply to everything else about me - be it cancer, poor personal finances or a mistake made - tolerance of what is, followed by action in the present moment to help make my continuing journey better.

A reckless driver speeds through a red light and crashes into Byron's car. First Byron accepts that it has happened - a karmic encounter between his path and the other driver's. It cannot be now "undone", so he does not waste his mental energy wishing that it should not have happened. He does not blame the other driver, since blame does not reverse the accident. And he does not get into a verbal encounter with him (tolerance). Having accepted what is, he objectively proceeds to do what the society he lives in requires be done in these circumstances, for example, exchange insurance information (action). And so do tolerance and action work in harmony for all other inter-personal issues, to ensure peaceful movement through life for oneself and one's fellow travelers.

A seemingly endless snowstorm disrupts the day's planned activities. We accept the uniqueness of a snowstorm, and its 'right' to be nothing else but a snow storm in the nature of things - it is neither bad, nor good. That also means we do not grumble or curse the storm. (Even if we do, the storm will continue until it finishes, and in the mean time we would have only increased our stress levels). That is tolerance of nature. Then we proceed to take action that is within our control - perhaps pick up the shovel and clear the driveway (and even hum a tune if we feel like it). And so should our attitude be, to all of nature, our unavoidable and often unyielding companion, if we are to make life's journey enjoyable.

Given the cumulative power of our (erroneous) past conditioning, all this may perhaps (initially) be hard work, but worth every bit of effort.

Tolerance and willful action - the practical derivatives of karma and the essential ingredients for a life of reduced stress, peace and progress towards our desired spiritual destination.

9

To Have or Not to Have

From craving arises sorrow
And from craving arises fear
If a man is free from craving,
He is free from fear and sorrow.

Dhammapada 216

We are advised, in Buddhist teachings, to get rid of *craving* (for things we like to have) and *clinging* (to what we already have), *because craving and clinging give rise to suffering,* sooner or later. Clinging and craving relate to *having.* But for daily living, we worldlings need to have some things. Thus, necessities for daily living on the one hand, and doctrinal advice on the other, may appear to pose a conflict in the mind of the keen traveler of Buddha's path, unless one can obtain a clear answer to the question "Where do I draw the line between wholesome and unwholesome having, so that I can progress towards the goal?" In other words, when am I craving and clinging and when am I not?

Dhammapada 204: "*Health is the greatest gain.* Contentment is the greatest wealth ....", helps towards finding that answer. If health is the greatest gain, then whatever acquisitions that help one to maintain a healthy life would be clearly wholesome (i.e., not driven by craving or clinging). The further away we get from that point, the more our attempts will fit closer into what is implied in Dhamma as craving and clinging. Why is health the greatest possession? Because without basic health of mind and body we simply will not be able to direct our energies, optimally, to progress on the spiritual path and thereby, to reach ultimate peace. Put in simpler and practical terms, this is to say that given health, contentment can follow. Let us now examine the subject of health a little further.

First, let us consider the health of the body. To maintain a healthy body we need nutritious food, physical activity, a shelter, affordability of health care and (protective) clothing, and the means needed to acquire these. That gives us the baseline from which to determine which possessions we need to ensure physical health.

Thus, a 'litmus test' to determine if a current possession or a planned acquisition is wholesome or unwholesome, is to ask oneself the question "Do I really need this to lead a healthy life, in body and mind?". If the answer is no, Buddhist premise would advise us to not acquire the new thing or let go of what we already have - it belongs elsewhere, hopefully to help or support another who is helpless to obtain for oneself the 'greatest gain' - health. Lived on that basis, there is plenty on this planet to meet the *real* needs of all.

To let go of what we cling to is indeed a difficult thing to do, because it has been conditioned (erroneously) into our very existence through our lifetime as well as through previous generations. But then, we need to understand the spiritual path is not easy, yet with proper effort it can be traversed. To reach a gemstone, first one has to go through the hard labor of digging what is above. Then come the fruits of labor.

Next, health of the mind. Here, both the prescription and the medicine-supreme is in the package called Buddha's Noble Eightfold Path.

To summarize, one could say that to desire and to have enough to provide for a healthy life is wholesome. That includes the needs of those one is absolutely responsible for due to their natural inability to fend for themselves, such as one's young children. Further away from that, we move deeper into the territory of craving and clinging. The means to wholesome having must always be, in Buddhist terms, 'right (livelihood)'.

Although in the final analysis clinging is a feature of the mind driven by the root cause of ignorance, it is helpful to subdivide clinging on the basis of the object clung to, i.e., (1) material things, (2) mental 'objects' - i.e., beliefs, values, ideas, labels and conventions etc. and (3) relationships. Any time one is suffering or is not feeling as happy as one wishes to be, invariably the immediate cause can be traced to clinging.

The opposite of clinging is letting go. So the therapy for dukkha is to let go - in Dhamma language, eradicate the craving, which itself is dependent on eradication of ignorance, the root cause.

Why does clinging cause dukkha? Because clinging means to hold onto something so it would stay (with us). But we cannot do that because the pivotal law of the universe says that everything changes, so that in clinging we stand in the path of movement (change). So we suffer. It is no different from the man who suddenly clings on to a moving train. Only a mad man or a drunkard would do that. The rest of us, witnessing such action and the tragic consequences, would perhaps think "What a fool!"

However, when we look at life, the rest of us are in the same plight. In our scenario, however, the action and consequences are not that obvious - in fact, they are often very subtle. We are all clinging to the massive train called Nature, which is for ever in motion, and we suffer heavily because of that clinging. Furthermore, to go deeper into Buddhist philosophy, we can say from the fact of *anatta* (no-self) that there is really no one to do the clinging after all. Thus we are wasting our life playing to an illusion by trying to cling, driven to satisfy an ego (self) that, in the final analysis, does not exist.

The discussion of the present subject will not be complete without answering the question "Is there anything at all one should crave for and cling to - for example, happiness?"

The answer to this is provided by Buddha's characteristically simple wording (but with profound meaning and enormous impact): "Cling not to that which changes". And what changes? Everything in the universe (as we worldlings perceive the universe to be). Thus, Buddha's words, for practical purposes may be restated: "Do not cling to *anything*." Included are happiness and unhappiness as they, too, are ever changing phenomena. All we can do, wisely, is to observe and let go. Just be aware, then let go. Difficult to do, but achievable and easier as we gather momentum on practice. And the reward? Peace.

The specific situation about craving for happiness is beautifully explained by Buddha via a simile[21]. A log floating down a river will eventually find its way to the free, open ocean only if the log does not cling to either bank. The story of our life is similar. The log is the mind. The river is life. One bank is unhappiness (dukkha) and the other is happiness (sukkha). The ocean is ultimate peace (Nibbana). If the mind does not cling to either unhappiness or happiness, then it will eventually reach ultimate peace.

---

[21] Samyutta Nikaya, 35:200 (Salayatana Samyutta sutta)

10

Self-Reliance

Therefore, O Ananda, take the Self as a lamp; take the Self as a refuge. Hold fast as a refuge to the truth. **Look not for refuge to anyone beside yourself. Work out your own salvation** with diligence.

- *Buddha* (Maha-Parinibbhana-Sutta)

Having traversed the Path of Deliverance to its destination, so advised the pioneer explorer, the Buddha, to another explorer Ananda who was eagerly seeking the same destination. In this gem of advice, the key message is *self-reliance*. If any efforts we ourselves take are to keep us on the right track, in the right direction and ensure progress, spiritually, then we should pay heed to Buddha's advice on self-reliance, which he emphasized throughout his teachings. All-round existential self-reliance is something that we need to develop, not partially or half-heartedly but with the utmost determination, full commitment and our iron will.

For purposes of discussing self-reliance within the context of this book we may think of the Noble Eightfold Path as comprising of two stages of development, that is mundane (worldly) and supra-mundane (higher spiritual) development. The latter relates to aspects such as meditation and are well documented in available existing literature. The former relates to aspects of ordinary day-to-day living such as livelihood, and seems to be inadequately addressed and was therefore chosen for treatment in the present chapter.

The importance of developing self-reliance in mundane aspects is easy to recognize. That is, if our minds are cluttered and pre-occupied with worry and anxiety, over ordinary issues of daily living, imposed by various types of mundane dependencies, would we have any space at all in our minds for higher spiritual development under the Noble Eightfold Path? The answer to that question, which is an obvious "No", explains why many 'Buddhists' do not have the time, energy, determination and patience to practice Dhamma. The solution therefore is for us to first develop the maximum possible self-reliance in every conceivable aspect of ordinary day-to-day living. That alone will eliminate the worries and anxieties that stand in the way of realization of our higher aspirations.

In passing let us note that it is much easier for monks to move onto higher spiritual practice because those factors (such as family responsibilities, ownership encumbrances and employment issues) which are the breeding grounds of obstacles (dependency) for the laypersons are by design not present in the traditional monastic life. So it is incumbent upon us laity to work harder than the monks to enter, and maybe even to maintain the momentum as we tread, the truly spiritual part of the Noble Eightfold Path.

It is harder to develop self-reliance in ordinary day-to-day living, than in higher spiritual living, because the former entails first *unlearning* and then learning, whereas the latter needs only learning. In mundane daily living we invariably are dependent on others or on worldly things, as a result of erroneous conditioning through lifetime. This is where we need to work hard to discard old habits of dependency and gradually let habits of self-reliance take their place. Unless we develop self-reliance in matters of mundane day-to-day living, we will find we are obstructed from proceeding to develop self-reliance at the spiritually higher levels. Thus, we may simply say that self-reliance at the mundane level is a pre-requisite for any meaningful spiritual development. So let us delve a little deeper into self-reliance at the mundane level of ordinary daily living. We will first discuss salient points about self-reliance in general. Then we will proceed to examine distinct areas of self-reliance where we may have problems and what we can do about them.

As a first point, let us recognize that dependency is rooted in the conditioned erroneous view that other people or external things are responsible for one's happiness and well-being. Such an attitude in adults, apart from being an obstacle to spiritual progress by creating dependency, is the main cause of all inter-personal problems in relationships, as it invariably results in blame and interference in others' affairs, and is even compounded when others have the same attitude. The diametrically opposite view, which is in touch with reality and healthy, is "I am responsible for my happiness and well-being." That is the Buddhist approach and the self-reliant way. It gets one moving on the Noble Eightfold Path. A person living according to that rational view, if capable of providing guidance to others, may provide such guidance *if and when asked for*, yet the actual work has to be done by the seeker.

Second, let us note that self-reliance is not something we can produce on demand when a crisis hits us. It has to be nurtured gradually over time and developed with patience, so when there is a crisis, we are already equipped to cope, with calmness of mind.

Third, it would be useful to recognize that a great aid to self-reliance is a life that is simple because simplicity implies fewer things in one's life to depend on. (Hence the intended and built-in simplicity of a monk's life.)

Fourth, the only true and lasting antidote for loneliness is not the presence of other people, but self-reliance.

As a last point let us note that while self-reliance is something we develop for ourselves, and that implies lack of dependency on others (adults), we can in reverse compassionately help others to be independent of *us*. Since the other person's self-reliance, which in this case we have facilitated, helps that person to accelerate his/her own journey on the Noble Eightfold Path, our action can only be considered as good karma that will bring merit to ourselves too.

Now let us examine some distinct aspects of self-reliance. For practical purposes we may view our dependencies as falling in three areas: (1) *physical* (2) *livelihood*, and (3) *mental* dependencies. Let us now examine each type in some detail.

Physical self-reliance. The most important aspect here is what one does to maintain one's body in optimum health. Instead of living an unhealthy lifestyle and being dependent regularly on the health-care system including the family doctor, medications, and care-givers at home, we can help ourselves enormously through regular exercise, proper nutrition and by doing our utmost to manage our daily stresses. The cost of healthy exercise is almost negligible. Activities such as a daily brisk walk for 30 minutes, a swim or bicycling are within the reach of all of us. So is healthy eating that is composed of a balanced diet of variety which includes grain products, vegetables, milk products and sources of protein. Maintaining healthy body weight becomes an easy task with proper exercise and nutrition. The cumulative benefit we receive from these inexpensive practices of preventive healthcare is far greater than that we can receive from any medication, medical help or any combinations of these anywhere on earth.

All the above is not to say that we can prevent all illness, decay and death. The law of impermanence still prevails, but while alive, we can live each day with the optimum health potentially available to each one of us. That is, without being a burden on externals, with the utmost self-reliance and enabling our minds to focus on the important task of spiritual growth and deliverance rather than spending mental energies on aches and pains. However, if we do have physical maladies already, then we still can provide much help for the rest of the physical self, with practices of self-reliance.

Besides taking care of the health of our bodies, we need to look at a long array of physical things and activities on which we are dependent, the non-availability of which has the potential to cripple us. A simple example is the total dependency of one spouse on another for meals or other mundane household affairs. Another common example is the continuing dependency of children grown to adulthood, on their parents for things that were only appropriate when they were younger.

Self-reliance for livelihood. This aspect of self-reliance, if not developed, can leave a potential 'time-bomb', particularly in difficult times like the present. It can be apparent where a bread-winner is dependent on one employer, or one type of career, or on dwindling resources for one's sustenance. It is also present in situations where one spouse is totally dependent on the other, where serious accident, separation, death or other changes may leave the dependent person helpless in the event the change does happen. In some such cases of dependency there is also the potential that the dependent person may have to live in subjection to, and at the mercy of, the giver, which in turn would lead to disruptive stress for the dependent person.

In all these cases the solution is to prepare oneself for eventualities by developing self-reliance. Thus, as an example take the case of the spouse who is dependent on the other for daily sustenance. No one can predict what the future holds for any relationship - the earning spouse may lose the job, there can be incapacitation due to an accident and so on. Therefore it is wise for the dependent spouse to take steps to develop the *potential* to earn a living, if not actual earning just now, for example by enrolling in a part-time study program in a subject area where the opportunities for earning a livelihood are good.

Mental self-reliance. This can manifest in a number of ways. First consider emotional dependence. When we were infants and children it made sense to be emotionally dependent on others (specially parents), but is not valid in the adult world. Nevertheless, there are many of us who have been unable to grow out of that dependency. One very common example of an erroneous belief, which causes this emotional dependency to continue, is that one, as an adult, *needs* love and praise from others to feel good. Another common mistaken belief is that it is terrible to be alone. Here we need to ponder over the erroneous views and replace them with the corresponding right views - this can be achieved most effectively via mindfulness meditation.

Another aspect of mental self-reliance is to refrain from depending on others such as family members, work colleagues and friends do the thinking and making decisions for oneself. It is also important to nurture one's intellectual growth by being open to new ideas instead of stagnating with the familiar, and to explore the unknown and mysteries of the universe wisely, though maybe cautiously.

A general strategy for developing self-reliance is as follows. For each area ask "On whom or on what external thing am I dependent and for what purpose?" and write down the answer on paper. Next dig deep into your mental resources and obtain specific answers to the question "What can I do to eliminate these dependencies (to be self-reliant)?" and again write the answers. Then, most importantly, proceed without postponement to DO what has been identified as needing to be done -- this *doing*, as always, is the most crucial part of our self-development.

For example, a sedentary person now bent on self-improvement recognizes a chronic dependency on doctors and medications for ordinary day-to-day health and to feel good. This person has identified that, to be self-reliant in this aspect he/she can (1) walk 30 minutes per day and (2) enroll in a nutrition course at the community college to learn the latest facts on healthy nutrition and (3) potentially benefit from a certain stress management book that helped a friend. By the end of the following week, this person has enrolled in the nutrition course, has bought the book on stress management, read it and begun to practise effective stress management techniques and exercises five days a week. It will not be long before this person has moved from dependency on the doctor and medications to self-reliance for ordinary day-to-day well-being -- a giant step forward.

Another example, is the person who, dependent for his/her daily living on an unstable employment, tries one's own business on a part-time basis as a fall-back so that if the need arises, the person is better prepared to cope.

Thus far we have examined how self-reliance can be developed in our mundane day-to-day existence, as a prerequisite for higher spiritual endeavors. Once we are past that hurdle, we can develop self-reliance for onward progress on the Path, which subject is addressed in later chapters (to the extent allowed by the objective of the present book.)

If we are to undertake a long journey to a wonderful destination in another continent, we will obviously need a suitable means of transportation that will take us to that destination. On a spiritual scale, the Noble Eightfold Path entails such a journey, the destination being Nibbana. Here our means of transportation is self-reliance. There is no other way to reach the destination.

11

Right and Wrong Views

What we are today comes from our thoughts of yesterday, and our present thoughts build our life of tomorrow: our life is the creation of our mind.

- From Dhammapada 1

It is best to start this topic with the reader pondering over the question "At a given moment in time, what is my existential (non-physical) essence (or in simpler terms), my personality?"

The answer to that question, for our present purpose, may be stated: "It is made up of two parts, namely,

1. an inherited part, which may be subdivided into

   • genetic inheritance,
   • karmic inheritance, and

2. accumulated views from birth to the present time."

Genetic material is passed down through one's lineage in a physical format, that is, via the genes. Examples of our genetic inheritance are skin color, physical appearance and predisposition to certain disorders such as hemophilia. Generally, our genetic inheritance is something we have to learn to live with, or cope with - we do not seem to have much of a choice there.

Science has recently begun to experiment, and sometimes tamper, with genetic material. We will not get into a discussion of that involved subject here except to say that these efforts may bring some benefits to alleviate sicknesses but human beings will never be able to alter the fundamental facts of aging and death, simply because they are manifestations of the primary law of the universe - impermanence.

While one's genetic material is passed through other people, karmic inheritance is purely one's own. Unlike the genes, karma is not passed in physical format - at least not physical in the way we perceive things as physical through our senses - but rather in the nature of energy vibrations[22]. Yet, karma influences genetic inheritance, to the extent that Buddhist doctrine teaches that one's karma will determine where one is to be born.

The consequence of past karma is something one has to live with and live through. Therefore, with regard to unwholesome past karma, it is wise to do whatever we have to do without complaint and resistance, pay back dues and 'get it over with' to help us with our onward journey with no more hindrance. What we do not pay back now will have to be paid back with interest later, like bank loans. For that reason, if I have to move garbage to make a living and for some personal reason I don't like doing it (though intrinsically there is nothing wrong with moving garbage), I might as well teach myself now to change my attitude and do it with acceptance and contentment. Why? Because the karma created by myself alone, and no other, placed me in a situation where I have to move garbage. While engaged in moving garbage to earn a living, if I so desire I can use the power of my *present* karma to take action to change my lot, with wisdom and patience. The same holds true for all kinds of other unpleasantness we have to go through in life, including tragedies.

What makes criminals or Buddhas out of us, or anything in between are primarily our views; and views are also the only things we have the power to alter, to change the direction of our existence. Hence the reason why 'purification of the mind (views)' becomes the essence of Buddhism. Therefore, the subject of real interest to us in the present chapter is *the accumulated views from birth to the present time. Views* is a general term we are using here to include concepts, ideas, prejudices, biases and any other entities akin to those. Just as we have acquired these since birth, we can also get rid of them when necessary (though with greater effort), if we develop the necessary skills to do so.

The first question we need to answer is how we acquire these views. We get them from the many influential environments we grow up in, or associate with, at different stages of our lives. These include our parents, the rest of the immediate family, relatives, our community, clergy, educational institutions and various other formats of society. We should also include inanimate information sources such as books and, in today's world, communications media such as television. The greatest influence on inculcation of views will be during our formative years.

---

[22] The distinction between matter and energy becomes hazy as we proceed to look at things at deeper sub-atomic levels.

The views we acquire may have significance in our own community, but may not be true in an absolute sense. Let us explore that proposition further with an example, which will also throw some new light on a factor of prime importance in Buddhist philosophy which we encountered earlier - that of no-self *(anatta)*.

Let us say a baby girl is just born. She is given the name Amy. Amy is an arbitrary 'fixture' we assign to the baby due to societal needs, and for the rest of her life she will be referred to by that name, so that she becomes permanently anchored to the 'fixture' Amy. This is just one of a multitude of anchors that will 'fix' Amy as another self - for example that she is the granddaughter of Burton (anchor 2) and Aretha (anchor 3). Amy lives at 2261 Clearwater Crescent (anchor 4) and so on, to an endless number of anchors (fixtures) - all our own creations, to serve some purpose of our worldly existence.

The net effect of this multiple anchoring is that Amy and others perceive her as an abiding self. But we know from our thorough analysis in earlier chapters that Amy is an incessantly changing entity and there is no abiding self in that entity. This, then, is the dilemma created by the anchoring to the fixtures. While that process helps to fill a societal need, it leads to the wrong view of an abiding ego (self). The belief in a self that initially was triggered by external influences (anchors) will become so ingrained in Amy as she grows up that it will be second-nature to her. Everything she does and perceives will be colored by that wrong view of self, now an influence of which she is not even aware. The only way in which this wrong view can be uprooted in the adult Amy is through un-learning, with the help of meditation, as we other adults too are painstakingly attempting to do.

What are generally referred to as wrong views in Buddhism are (1) the view of an abiding self, (2) view of permanency of things and (3) all corollaries that follow from (1) and (2). Let us look at a sampling of wrong views and the corresponding right views organized in a table format below, essentially reflecting the majority of the key points discussed in the previous chapters. They are stated here in simple language and somewhat differently to the manner in which they are presented in doctrinal writings[23]- in order to focus on their application to day-to-day living.

---

[23] Readers interested in a study of the classical description may consult " The Discourse on *The All-Embracing Net of Views:* The Brahmajala Sutta and its Commentaries" translated from the Pali by Bhikkhu Bodhi. Buddhist Publication Society, 1978 and "*The Discourse on Right View:* The Sammadithhi Sutta and Its Commentaries" translated from the Pali by Bhikkhu Nanamoli, revised by Bhikkhu Bodhi, BPS 1992.

Table 1: Right and Wrong Views

A	B
Wrong View (Worldly)	**Right View** (Transcendental)
View of permanence	All things are impermanent (subject to change). Some change slowly, some rapidly. *(Impermanence)*
View of an abiding self (ego)	There is no abiding self. No 'I', 'me' 'mine' etc. These are mere conventional terms used for communication *(Egolessness)*
It would be possible to sustain happiness with sensory gratification	Sensory stimuli sometimes result in transient pleasures but invariably lead to unhappiness when the stimuli cease. *(Impermanence)*
I should welcome praise and be averse to blame	I should be unaffected by praise and blame as both are transient[24]. *(Impermanence)*
The world is responsible for my suffering.	I am responsible for both my happiness and suffering. *(Karma)* The root-cause of my suffering is my own ignorance. *(Dependent Origination).*
I should not be having dukkha	Physical dukkha is inherent in change (impermanence) and so I have to accept it. Some physical dukkha may be temporarily abated, but eventually I will have to face physical dukkha. Mental dukkha can be eliminated by replacing ignorance (wrong views) with wisdom (right views). *(Impermanence)*
My unpleasant feelings will not go away.	They will. Feelings (in fact all mental activities) are subject to impermanence. They change faster than constituents of the body. *(Impermanence)*

---

[24] "Even as a rock is not shaken by the wind, the wise man is not shaken by praise or blame." - Dhammapada 81

Table 1: Right and Wrong Views (continued)

A	B
Wrong View (Worldly)	**Right View** (Transcendental)
Key to happiness is amassing wealth.	Key to happiness is purification of the mind, that is, to move from ignorance to wisdom (Link 1 of *Dependent Origination*)
My mind and my body belong to me. So are my children, spouse and wealth.	They really belong to nature, and to me only in name[25] (convention). (*Egolessness*).
I should develop affection for my dear ones and they in turn should show affection to me. The rest of the world is not really important.	Affection for a select few (dear ones) causes attachment, which in turn brings suffering when parting occurs[26]. So develop unconditional love for *all*, including the 'dear ones.' It is a far superior love. (*Impermanence*)
Birth must be celebrated and death mourned.	Birth and death are equal concomitants of the Wheel of Life. Treat them as equals. Develop wisdom to transcend both. (*Impermanence*)
All I am going through is my fate. There is nothing I can do about it.	My past karma is a determinant of what I am going through. However I have the power to change the direction of my existence from this point on, in the way I generate fresh karma, that is, through action now. (*Karma*)
Some things (and people) in this world are good, others bad.	Everything in the world just *is* - neither bad nor good. Good and bad are human labels (conventions). Cause and effect chains have brought things to what and where they are. (*Impermanence and karma*).

[25] " 'These are my sons. This is my wealth.' In this way the fool troubles himself. He is not even the owner of himself: how much less of his sons and his wealth." - Dhammapada 62

[26] "From affection springs grief, from affection springs fear; for him who is wholly free from affection there is no grief, much less fear." - Dhammapada 213

The above list is not exhaustive, yet it is a significant part of a very long list of right and wrong views that we can compose to cover every imaginable facet of human existence. The list of examples reveals clearly that every one of our views can be carefully examined to see if it is right or wrong. If it is a wrong view, the corresponding right view can always be deduced in terms of two of the three basic facts of existence - impermanence *(anicca)* and egolessness *(anatta)*. Karma and Dependent Origination, which we have used above to explain some views, are in the final analysis themselves dependent on impermanence. The reader may add to this list as he/she progresses through his/her studies of Dhamma, as the list will become valuable preparatory material for Vipassana meditation. Let us now observe a few insights using the information in Table 1.

1. The Worldly Way and Transcendental Way. To live with the views of Column A is worldly living - living plagued by confusion and dukkha. It is the life of sensory gratification, with transient pleasures that fade, leaving behind dukkha. Living according to the views of Column B is the transcendental path, the way that leads to permanent peace - the Dhamma way. Our problems cannot be solved in the world of Column A, because that is where the problems are - we are submerged in dukkha there and we cannot see. So, like the Coast Guard pilot who leaves the host ship and flies the rescue helicopter above the ocean to find a missing person, we have to step out into world B (in our mind) and look at what is happening in world A to understand, and find solutions, for our dukkha. That is Buddha's way and needless to say, it goes exactly opposite to the worldly way we are accustomed to. Hence the inherent difficulty in moving from the latter to the former.

2. The Worldly Views Inculcated into Us Prepared Us to Undergo Dukkha. It is clear from the examples in Table 1 that as we were growing up we were not taught views based on the basic facts of existence (impermanence and egolessness). On the contrary we were taught to do practically everything to support the ego and on the illusion that things, particularly those that we like, remain more or less unchanged. Few, if any, amongst us grew up truly understanding the realities of *anicca* and *anatta.*

For example, how many of us grew up being able to treat death as an event occupying a place in par with birth? We learnt to celebrate birth and abhor death. The result? The irrational Fear One, that of death. On the other hand, think of the immense peace we would have in life if we could have learnt to interact with a person with unconditional love *(metta)* while alive, and then when the person dies, to treat the passing away with equanimity? After all, in the eyes of impermanence the passing away of a human being is no different to the passing away of a seasonal flowering plant, say the petunia, as the summer comes to an end. What is born *has to* die (and that includes ourselves). To be in touch with reality (and therefore to be really at peace) we need to accept that fact. Then our actions and feelings relating to human death should, ideally be no different from those we demonstrate at the passing away of the petunia. But we cannot act in that manner because of the deep-rooted erroneous views (conditioning) that now control our emotions involuntarily, until we have been able to eradicate them with intensive Vipassana meditation.

As another example, take the case of praise and blame. How wonderful life would be if we could live unaffected by both praise and blame, except for judiciously selecting constructive feedback to enhance our growth. Instead we are usually on an emotional roller-coaster driven by our sensitivity to what others think of, or say to, us. Again this is the way we were taught to view praise and blame.

In general, how many of us can truly claim that our lives are based on *all* views akin to those in column B and similar transcendental views on other issues of life that are not listed? If we do, we don't need this struggle to master and practise Dhamma!

3. Be Here Now. In our readings on Buddhism we often encounter advice on the need to live in the present moment or, to use a popular phrase, to 'be here now.' This is because it is only in the present moment that our senses are active and we can interact with reality. The past, though perhaps real when it happened to be the present, is now totally imagination. Likewise, though the future may turn out to be real when it becomes the present, it is at the moment total imagination. So it makes sense to live in the present moment and be in touch with reality. However, our discussion on views so far reveals a very important additional factor. Since views can be right or wrong, we need to process the present-moment information of the world received through our senses with *right* views, not wrong views if we are to 'see things as they really are.'

Thus, in the example we had about Cousin Burl in Chapter 7 'Our Sensory World', Bertram developed an aversion towards him because of wrong views (as in Column A). However, if Bertram perceives him through right views (as in Column B), then he will see the reality about Cousin Burl and, instead of being averse, he will be compassionate towards Burl. So our formula for living in the present moment is not 'be here now' but ' be here now *with right views.*'

4. Conventional Reality and Absolute Reality. Except for the few actions such as eating and breathing needed for survival, our ordinary day-to-day living centers on a vast array of conventions (rules, guidelines, names, labels, symbols, values etc.) *of our own making.* In contrast, absolute reality refers to things as they are in Nature and outside of convention created by people. For example, consider the proliferation of anniversary dates we have to live with - Mother's Day, Father's Day, Grandparent's Day, birthdays, Halloween Day, Boxing Day and so on. Promoted endlessly by commercial interests, these days have come to be significant events in our hectic worldly lives, though often turning out to be mechanical routines after some time. In the eyes of absolute reality all these days are the same - just another sunrise.

Convention is useful, necessary and only valid for the purpose, or society or geographical area, and the time frame, for which it is made. Thus Adrienne, a 100 mph speed, money, a beautiful hairstyle, oxcart, a good man, accountant and tragedy are all examples of the endless list of conventions, that we created to live by.

Absolute reality has no judgments, boundaries or time limits. In contrast, when viewed through convention, we pass judgment on the world, usually labeling as good or bad. Thus, a "crooked tree" makes sense within convention, but does not exist in an absolute sense. The tree exists as a part of nature, not as a *crooked* tree. "Crooked" is a unilateral judgment we human beings try to impose on nature (on absolute reality). Though it satisfies us, nature moves on totally unaffected and aloof - it will probably make the offspring of the crooked tree also a crooked tree, in spite of what we think or say! Likewise, the need to arrange dinnerware on the dining table according to a specific layout is simply convention, but in an absolute sense it has no meaning. And so it is with all convention.

Many of our problems and suffering in life arise not because of conventions, but because we fail to realize that (1) for every conventional reality there is an absolute reality, (2) there is a fundamental difference between the two realities, often being opposites and (3) while conventional reality is needed for our transient existence within transient societal boundaries, it is absolute truth that matters for progress on the spiritual path and attainment of final peace. It is also the lack of this same realization that causes one to think that his convention is right, the other's is wrong and therefore the justification to impose one's convention on the other. And that happens to be the root cause of all our conflicts and confrontations, whether it be between two individuals, two ethnic groups or two countries.

5. No One Can be Blamed for Our Wrong Views. Views that we acquire as we grow up are not all wrong, but generally most are. We cannot blame anyone for inculcating wrong views in us simply because they were ignorant as we are. Most people do what they do with good intentions but also through ignorance - the mix of ignorance to wisdom is unique to each one of us. They taught us what they knew. We taught and continue to teach what we know. If the 'teacher' is ignorant, what is imparted is ignorance. If the 'teacher' is wise, what is imparted is wisdom. That is the way things are. The only way to brake the vicious cycle is to recognize our ignorance and work diligently to eradicate our dukkha with the help of the precious gift that Buddha left for us - the unsurpassed Dhamma.

Every generation, through ignorance, passes on wrong views to the next. Most of us will find that by the time we got around to insightfully grasp Dhamma, we have already passed on wrong views to those we influenced and now they are outside our range of influence for corrective action. So they in turn pass on wrong views to their next generation and the cycle continues. No wonder 2500 years have elapsed since Buddha passed away, yet we as a generation are in the same predicament of illusion as the ignorant people who lived in Buddha's time. However, in each generation, "there are beings whose eyes are only a *little* covered with dust; they will understand the truth[27] " and they sustain the relay to keep the flame of Dhamma from being extinguished for ever.

---

[27] Buddha (from Majjhima Nikaya 26)

12

Calming the Mind
(Samatha Meditation)

The mind is fickle and flighty, it flies after fancies wherever it likes; it is difficult to restrain. But it is a great good to control the mind; a mind self-controlled is a source of great joy.

Dhammapada 35

Before we embark on a discussion of Buddhist meditation, let us do a very simple exercise. Pick a small object (a pencil, pen, cup - anything) with your hand, look at it and put it away. Then close your eyes and for the next ten minutes try to focus your attention on the mental image of that object. For timing, use a clock or wristwatch alarm or just do it by feel. Whenever you stray away from that image, try to bring back the concentration to the object.

What is the most striking thing that we notice during the exercise? It is that the mind does not stay focused on the object. It wanders as it fancies - to sounds, bodily pains, other thoughts and so on. It is like a constantly rebellious child. Unless we are already accomplished meditators, this problem is universal, because that is the way the mind is. It jumps from thought to thought because by habit that is what it knows, and likes, to do. The purpose behind *Samatha* meditation is to tame this discursive mind, gently guiding it to focus its attention on one object.

The principle that Samatha meditation capitalizes on is the scientific fact that the mind cannot think of two things at the same time (that is during the same 'thought moment'). So when we induce the mind to think of a neutral object such as the breath, then during each thought moment of that thinking process it cannot think of other things which agitate it. Through repetition of that process, when we succeed in guiding the mind to concentrate on one thing at the exclusion of all else for a reasonable length of time, the net effect is calming of the mind. The level of tranquillity (calmness) realized will be a stark contrast to the usual state of the mind resulting from its habitual discursiveness. Of course, a calmed mind leads to calming of many bodily activities (such as lowering of blood pressure) and one's entire life rhythm, contributing to better overall health. Note that concentration (on the chosen object) is the practice; calmness is the result.

Buddhist meditation comprises two types, Samatha, which as we have seen develops calmness through concentration and *Vipassana* which enables one to perceive things without distortion ('see things as they are'). For optimum effectiveness, Vipassana needs a mind that is calm, which is a mind that has been prepared by Samatha. Thus Samatha meditation is a prerequisite for effective Vipassana meditation, if one is intent on realizing the best results with the latter. Vipassana will be discussed in some detail in the next two chapters.

The objects of focus available for Samatha practice are many. We will use our natural breath as the object and restrict our discussion and practice to that, to keep things simple. The breath is one of the most popular objects of meditation and was used by Buddha himself the night of his enlightenment. The main advantage in using the breath is its natural (guaranteed) availability twenty-four hours a day for a lifetime, so that one does not have to depend on externals for objects of meditation. Another advantage is that it could also be used as a model and a 'home base' for Vipassana (mindfulness) practice.

Meditation carried out with the breath as the object of focus is called *anapanasati* in Pali, *sati* meaning mindfulness (and *ana* and *apana* meaning inhalation and exhalation respectively). So strictly speaking, anapanasati is mindfulness of breathing. However, it is common practice to use the term anapanasati when referring to breathing meditation, whether it is used for Vipassana practice or for Samatha.

The procedure for the Samatha (anapanasati) meditation is as follows:

- Sit comfortably in the cross-legged position (if you are comfortable with this posture) or simply in a chair with hands cupped and resting on the lap. Keep the back straight with the chin drawn in slightly. Breathe normally and close the eyes.

- With awareness note the in-breath and out-breath as they pass through the tip of the nostrils, as a security guard watches people entering and leaving a building through the main door. Do not follow the breath into the body or out of the body.

- Each time the mind is distracted by a thought, simply acknowledge that (with no aversion or craving) and gently come back to the anchor, the breath at the tip of the nostrils. Do this with patience however many times necessary.

- Practice for ten minutes the first day and very gradually increase the duration to a maximum of an hour (usually considered to be an optimal duration), the increase in duration being determined by your own estimation of how comfortable you feel with the progress.

That is all there is to the essentials of Samatha practice. Now we will cover some noteworthy points of clarification regarding the practice.

1. Distractions. The mind *is* going to wander into other thoughts. That is the nature of the untrained mind and that is also the very reason why we have undertaken Samatha practice. So we must accept the discursiveness of the mind and after acknowledging the distraction, gently return to the breath. In accepting its wandering nature, we are for the first time beginning to understand the nature of our own mind, which is a great step in itself. It may help the meditator to mentally note any negative distractions as "physical dukkha" or " mental dukkha" and any feelings of joy as "sukkha" and get back to the breath. After the meditator has acquired some mastery over the practice, this supplementary aid of labeling could be eliminated.

2. Counting. Counting the breath could help the beginning meditator to better stay focused on the breath. There are many ways of counting, but for our present purpose the following is suggested. Count the first breath as "one, one". That is, "one" at in-breathing, "one" at out-breathing. Count the second breath as "two, two". The third breath as "three, three" and so on up to "ten, ten". Do not count beyond "ten, ten" as the attention then tends to get diverted to numbers rather than the breath; instead start all over again at "one, one". A very effective alternative to counting is to use the word "Buddho". Use "Bud" at in-breathing and "dho" at out-breathing.

3. Absorptions. When the concentration becomes sufficiently deep, the meditator will notice a sign *(nimitta* in Pali) arising, as a mental image. This may take the form of a puff of smoke, a cloud, an image of Buddha, a gentle touch of a breeze or some other form, indicative of peacefulness. The arising of this mental image is an indication that the meditator has reached the stage of calmness called 'neighborhood concentration' (*upacara-*

samadhi in Pali). This stage is the entry 'door' leading to two paths, one of which must be chosen by the meditator at this point. One path leads to various higher stages of 'absorptions' or ecstatic trances (*jhanas* in Pali), intensifying the tranquillity realized so far - this path[28] is really continuation of Samatha. The trances will enable the meditator to enjoy spiritual 'highs' which are *transient*. However, they will not take the person one step closer to liberation from dukkha. The other path is Insight or Mindfulness (*Vipassana*) meditation, which alone is the way to deliverance from dukkha. Our interest, in the context of this book, is the Vipassana route, discussed in the next two chapters.

4. Place and time of day. It helps to select a place that is quiet, as Samatha meditation is an exercise in concentration. The ideal is a quiet room where you are the only occupant. When this is not possible, meditating in a group is fine, so long as everyone maintains silence. With experience and proficiency, the meditator will be able to practise even within noise and common distractions. Silence is very important for beginning meditators. With regard to time of day, it is best to allocate a specific time for meditation practice and adhere to that time slot daily, so that meditation becomes part of one's routine like dinner.

5. Effort. The effort applied in Samatha meditation is mental only and minimal. All the effort needed is to gently bring the thinking (concentration) back from a discursive thought to the breath at the tip of the nostrils. This is where Samatha meditation primarily differs from *Pranayama* of Yoga practice, where physical effort is applied on the breath and respiratory system to alter the characteristics of one's breath. In *anapanasati* we use the breath itself as is.

6. Results. Since meditation is an art in 'going with the flow', one must not expect anything from the practice. The only rule for successful meditation is: start and continue. If you look for results and do not find it, you get restless and defeat the purpose of the exercise. Don't look for tranquillity. When the time is up, tranquillity will come as a reward for your doing your part with consistency and dedication. Remember, the initial part of any significant change is allowing the body and mind to get used to a new habit. The mind has been used to running amok all this time and we are trying to teach it to stay still and focus on just one thing. It is like learning to drive a standard car after being used to driving an automatic or learning touch typing after being used to one-finger typing.

---

[28] Those interested in pursuing the subject of jhanas may consult the book *The Jhanas in Theravada Buddhist Meditation* by Mahathera Henepola Gunaratana (Wheel Publication No. 351/353, Buddhist Publication Society, 1988)

It takes time to change any habit and the same principle applies to the way the mind behaves.

Do not be concerned as to the number of minutes you have been able to focus on the breath. Each single thought-moment you are able to focus on the breath is a moment of peace for the mind. So go by the smaller thought-moments, not minutes.

Finally, do not compare your performance with that of others. Meditation is unique to the individual because each mind is unique. There is no competition or comparison in meditation. When you reach enlightenment, only you will know because it all happens inside *your* mind.

13

A Preparatory Technique

for Vipassana Meditation

The objective of Vipassana meditation is to perceive things without distortion. Put differently, we can say that we want to perceive with right views the things we now perceive with wrong views. This is realized in two stages, namely:

(1) an *intellectual understanding* of precisely what the wrong view is, and also what the corresponding right view is (that is, 'right understanding' in formal Buddhist terms), and

(2) an *experiential* right view realized as deep meditative insight, the prerequisite for which is the intellectual understanding gained in (1)

In this chapter we will become familiar with a technique that has been successfully tried by me and by students in my meditation classes, to implement the first stage. In addition to serving the desired purpose of an effective stepping-stone for Vipassana practice, the technique was found to provide significant healing benefits on its own, even before we moved on to, and practised, the corresponding experiential phase of Vipassana. Remember, though, that this activity is only *complementary* , and a prerequisite, to stage (2), which is the vehicle for reaching the ultimate goal of the practice.

The technique takes the form of written work, for which the worksheet form shown below has shown to be most effective. The steps of the method are as follows:

(1) Select an aspect of dukkha that you are currently experiencing and write this down clearly in box (A) in simple language, as if you are speaking to your best friend. It is important this description focuses on *feelings* and not views (thoughts).

(2) In box (B) write down the worldly *views* that circulate involuntarily in your mind in connection with this particular dukkha. Here one must write the *views* (and not feelings). Leave space below each worldly view for a further entry, as described in the next step.

(3) Refer to Table 1 in Chapter11: Right and Wrong Views and select transcendental views that rebut the worldly view. If Table 1 does not list the transcendental views for your particular situation, deduce your own from the principles of impermanence *(anicca),* egolessness *(anatta),* Dependent Origination *(Paticcasamuppada)* and cause and effect *(karma).* If necessary, go back to the relevant chapters and read up again on these subjects.

Enter the transcendental views in the space below the worldly view. This is the most important step. You have just rebutted, in a down-to-earth practical way, the dukkha-causing worldly thinking with transcendental thinking based on Buddha's Dhamma and you have taken a giant step towards attaining peace on this particular dukkha. Compare the two views contemplatively for a moment.

(4) Repeat steps (2) and (3) for all other worldly views associated with this particular dukkha.

Whenever this specific dukkha bothers you during the day, read over what you have written in the worksheet, particularly the transcendental views. As you do this repeatedly, you will feel the dukkha abating partially, yet significantly (with the completion to be achieved with Vipassana practice), as the mind gets calmed by the wisdom of Dhamma. A degree of relief is felt. It is as though Buddha's divine influence suddenly appears in our irrationally thinking mind and imbues it with rationality and wisdom. In fact, what we have done is to allow Dhamma to penetrate our mind, since Buddha is not with us today to help us in person.

It is important that this preparatory technique be carried out *on paper* as we discussed, and not just mentally. The reason is we want to *focus* on our views, but the mind has not yet been trained to focus properly. So, by writing things on paper, we are forcing the otherwise discursive mind to stay focused during the exercise. In that sense, we can think of this technique as *temporarily* serving a key purpose of Samatha, that is, the prerequisite for Vipassana. Yet, it is not a complete substitute for Samatha, so that we should practise Samatha too daily, with the eventual goal to master it. With intensive Samatha practice carried over a period of time, when we begin to feel we are adept at keeping the mind focused as long as we want, then we can discontinue this technique.

Worksheet

(A) STATEMENT OF MY DUKKHA:

(B) ASSOCIATED VIEWS

Worldly View 1:

Transcendental Views:

Worldly View 2

Transcendental Views:

Worldly View 3:

Transcendental Views

Let us illustrate the technique with two examples. To keep things simple, we will use two cases that we referred to earlier, that of Alicia's lower back pain (in chapter 6: "Focus on Dukkha") and Bertram's aversion towards Cousin Burl (in chapter 7: "Our Sensory World"). The first is an individual problem and the second relational. Let us first state the situations briefly.

Example 1. Alicia recently suffered some severe lower back pains. After medical diagnosis, the doctor reported that she has a slipped disk. The doctor explained the possible courses of action, but Alicia became apprehensive.

Example 2. Bertram's relationship with Cousin Burl has been unpleasant right through. He feels Burl is selfish, mean and obnoxious. Burl visited Bertram's family recently. After meeting Burl, once again Bertram was fuming with anger. He continued to be upset even after Burl left.

Example 1 (Worksheet as filled by Alicia)

(A) STATEMENT OF MY DUKKHA:

I feel worried and hopeless after the news of the medical diagnosis.

(B) ASSOCIATED VIEWS

Worldly View 1: Why me?

Transcendental Views:
1. Dukkha is universal and has not exclusively chosen me. Dukkha appears in different forms to different persons and so also to the same person at different times. Dukkha has to be faced right through life - it is inevitable because of the law of impermanence and my own past karma. I can think of many other situations which could have brought much greater dukkha upon myself. So, I have to *accept* the physical dukkha of the slipped disk but I need not overburden myself with *mental* dukkha entertaining irrational views such as "Why me?"
    (Impermanence and karma)

Worldly View 2: I should have been more careful in the way I used my body in the past; if I did, this would not have happened.

Transcendental Views:
1. Things happen exactly the way they are supposed to. Any happening is determined by an unfathomable cause-effect linkage that goes back in endless time. So I cannot blame myself for what I did or didn't do up until now. Neither can I visit the past to change what has happened. And I could only do what I knew to do at each moment in my life.
    (Dependent Origination, past karma)
2. However I can take the most sensible action in the present moment to improve things, including a thorough discussion with the doctors.
    (Present karma)

After Consulting Medical Professionals:
3. Now I have the following possibilities from which to choose a plan for recovery, subject to discussion with my family and supplementary medical consultation:
    a. Bed rest for a number of weeks, and pain relieving drugs when necessary - to be later followed by wearing a corset or supportive collar. This may turn out to be all I need for full recovery.
    b. If (a) fails and compression on the nerve root produces muscle weakness (which is not present now), I can consider surgery to relieve the pressure.   *(Action - present karma)*

Things are , after all, not as bad as I thought earlier. Now I can see how I over-burdened myself with self-induced and unnecessary mental dukkha

Example 2 (Worksheet as filled by Bertram)

(A) STATEMENT OF MY DUKKHA:

I feel very angry and agitated after meeting Cousin Burl today.

(B) ASSOCIATED VIEWS

Worldly View 1: He shouldn't have visited us today.

Transcendental Views:
1. The changing nature of everything in the universe, including that of time, has put the incident behind us - it is past. My saying "he shouldn't have visited us today" a million times will not alter the fact that he visited us today.   *(Impermanence)*

2. For the same reason, given time, all that is now existing or happening (Cousin Burl, myself, and my feelings etc.) will come to pass - into insignificance. So why not think "This too will pass" at the present moment and unload the burden from my mind?   *(Impermanence)*

Worldly View 2   He has annoying ways.

Transcendental Views:
Each one of us 6 billion people on this planet has a unique make-up of right views (wisdom) and wrong views (ignorance) - which makes each person unique in one's ways. I am ignorant, just as Cousin Burl is, though may be on some different things. That is the way things are. Also my own karma placed me in a situation where he is my cousin. All of this tells me that I should show compassion to him, instead of being averse and angry. *(Dependent Origination, karma)*

Worldly View 3: He caused me to get angry.

Transcendental Views:
1. It's not others or their behavior that causes me to be upset, but how I perceive them. I need to identify, as I am doing now filling this form, the wrong views (ignorance) in me that caused me to get upset and with the help of Vipassana, gradually work to eradicate them.
    (Dependent Origination)
2. Anger first destroys the one who harbors it, like hot coal picked up with one's hands to be thrown at someone *(karma)*. Furthermore, if the one at whom it is directed is clever enough to duck, he escapes totally unscathed.

3. In absolute reality there is no 'me' to be upset. So why am I causing unnecessary mental dukkha for myself trying to protect a self that does not exist? *(Egolessness)*

It is clear that all we have done on the worksheet is put in writing right Dhammic views to counteract irrational worldly views in an organized manner. Thereby, we force the otherwise discursive mind to stay focused on the realities of the dukkha-causing issue. Remember that thoughts cause feelings, meaning our thoughts arise first and feelings follow from them. Hence wrong views cause dukkha and right views, sukkha (joy). Replacing wrong views with right views, as we have done in filling the worksheet, should help in our efforts to shift the feelings from dukkha to sukkha, or at least from dukkha to neutral feelings.

The technique indicated in these two illustrative examples can be applied to any other existential problem. To every imaginable human condition, we can find a solution, once we step out of worldly living and thinking. Then, we can come back to our worldly living armed with the solution for implementation.

In this chapter we have familiarized ourselves with an effective technique for the *intellectual understanding* of right views. That in itself is a beneficial and necessary step on the Path, yet it is a stepping stone. With the intellectual understanding alone we have not been able to eradicate the old erroneous views *from their roots* embedded in the deep crevices of the mind. Therefore, we need to move on to the second phase - the experiential realization of right view in order to obtain full benefits of our endeavor.

At this stage, the reader is encouraged to fill the worksheet form in respect of some of the evident dukkha he/she is encountering at present, for use in Vipassana practice, explained in the next chapter.

14

Using Vipassana

Better than a hundred years lived in ignorance, without contemplation, is one single day of life lived in wisdom and deep contemplation.

Dhammapada 111

In this chapter, we will discuss a fairly simple and practical way in which Vipassana meditation can be effectively used in daily living. Therefore, our objective is neither a classical[29] treatment of Vipassana nor an in-depth analysis of the subject aimed at attaining the higher reaches possible with Buddhist meditation, but a means to realize significant benefits in our ordinary daily living.

What is Vipassana, in practical terms? Let us start with an analogy. If a window glass is covered with dirt it will prevent us from getting a clear view of what is outside. In addition, in countries that experience sub-zero temperatures, patches of ice can form on the window glass, so we get a reduced view of the outside. Finally, when there is a wet snow fall on a windy day, a layer of snow can cover the glass. With all these impediments - the dust, the ice and the snow - we may hardly see the outside or we may get a hazy, distorted view. If we want to get a really clear view of the outside, we need to remove the impediments.

What invariably happens when we perceive things with our minds is similar to looking through that window. Here our impediments are wrong views - they are the dust, the ice and the snow of the mind. Our mind cleared of wrong views is like the glass that is cleared of the impediments. So the purpose of Vipassana meditation is to clear the mind of wrong views (by experiential means), in order that we have an undistorted view of nature, especially our existence. In other words, see reality. When we realize that, our minds are in harmony with nature and truth. Then there is

---

[29] The reader interested in pursuing an in-depth study and practice beyond the scope of the present book may consult *Satipatthana Vipassana:* Insight through Mindfulness and/or *Practical Insight Meditation:* Basic and Progressive Stages. Both are by Ven. Mahasi Sayadaw and are published by the Buddhist Publication Society.

no confusion, restlessness or worry. Instead, our minds becomes clear and peaceful.

The main difference in technique between Samatha and Vipassana practice is that in Samatha our objective is to keep the mind's attention focused on one object, whereas in Vipassana we let the mind move from object to object or event to event, but observe phenomena in the light of the basic facts of existence, namely impermanence, egolessness and dukkha.

Diligent and regular practice of Samatha meditation (Chapter 12) prepares the mind to concentrate deeply and makes it calm. This gives the mind the capability to penetrate what it looks at and see things that the mind cannot otherwise see, the way a microscope helps one to see the details of human tissue, which the naked eye cannot see. Furthermore, the preparatory technique described in Chapter 13 helps the mind to *intellectually* identify (a) wrong views through which we look at issues that confront us in our daily lives and (b) the corresponding right views. Armed with these two aids, the mind is prepared and ready to venture into its last hurdle - to *experientially* realize right view as deep meditative insight. Given diligent practice, this experiential practice alone will complete the process of dislodging the wrong views from their roots (and substitute right views in their place). Along with that, peace settles in as the root causes of agitation no more exist.

So, the complete sequence of Buddhist meditation can be listed, for our practical purposes, in four steps as follows:

1. An intellectual understanding of right and wrong views pertaining to the issues likely to come up during the meditation.

2. Breathing meditation (anapanasati) carried out in *Samatha mode* to bring the mind to the point of neighborhood concentration.

3. Breathing meditation carried out in *mindfulness mode* to prepare the breath as 'home base', and model, for Vipassana practice.

4. Mindfulness, one at a time, of *all objects and events* that the mind moves into in daily living. When we are done with one particular object or event, we can either proceed to the next object (or event) the mind moves into or go back to the 'home base', and repeat the process.

Now we will expand on these four steps to obtain a procedure and illustrate the application with examples.

Step 1: Intellectual understanding. The general background to this step was covered in Chapter 13. Review the chapter if needed, at least during the early days of practice. Go over the contents of worksheets of the two examples in that chapter and note the wrong (worldly) views and the right (transcendental) views. Also, go over the worksheets you filled in at the conclusion of Chapter 13 for evident dukkha *in your own life* and again note the wrong views and the right views with which you rebutted the former.

As you progress in practice over a reasonable period of time, this information will become familiar to you and the paper work can be gradually phased out.

Step 2: Reaching neighborhood concentration. This was described in Chapter 12. Practice anapanasati in Samatha mode (i.e., with the focus on breath) till you reach neighborhood concentration (appearance of a mental image[30] - *nimitta*). Now you are ready to move into mindfulness mode.

Step 3: Mindfulness of breath ('home base'). Instead of one-pointed focusing on the breath at the tip of the nostrils, we follow and contemplate on the whole breath with its movement, without imposing any restraints or force of even minimal intensity. In our deep contemplation we become mindful of:

- Impermanency *(anicca)* of the breath - there is first the birth of the in-breath, then there is a life span of that in-breath and then it dies. We note that what is born dies. What arises ceases. We note the same regarding the out-breath. We observe that the death of one (in-breath) gives rise to birth of another (out-breath). We note the arising of a full breath, its life span, cessation, death and the birth of another full breath. Insightfully, we realize that phenomena are in constant flux.

- Egolessness *(anatta).* We observe that the breathing happens as a process and does not belong to us, there is no abiding entity that it can belong to - it is a part of nature. We also note that there is no abiding entity within the breath itself (although we call it the 'breath' for purposes of communication.)

---

[30] While neighborhood concentration (a by-product of Samatha) is necessary as a prerequisite to gain *optimal* benefits from Vipassana, one can realize substantial benefits from it while still a beginning practitioner of Samatha. In other words, developing Samatha skills and practicing Vipassana can happen in parallel, though the effectiveness of the latter will be at a reduced level.

- *Dukkha*[31]. There is constant effort needed to support the breath and so there is dukkha associated with it.

- *Corollaries* that follow from the three basic facts. For example, we observe that we cannot hold on to an in-breath or out-breath, for we will die; we learn, therefore, that if we cling to things subject to the law of impermanence (and all conditioned things are), we have to suffer. So we understand the need to constantly let go of things.

Step 4: Mindfulness of objects/events. When we have established mindfulness of the breath (our 'home base'), then we follow the mind and be aware of whatever the mind moves on to - it can be an object (examples: a tree or a cloud or a person) or event (examples: a feeling of anger or pounding of ocean waves or the sound made by a lawnmower). We observe the phenomena in deep contemplation, insightfully realizing things in relation to the basic facts of existence - anicca, dukkha, anatta. The details of procedure are similar to those in step 3.

To illustrate, let us assume that each one of us meditators is Bertram of example 2[32] in Chapter 13. Sometime after we are mindfuly established on the breath, let us say our thoughts go to Cousin Burl resulting in feelings of aversion (anger etc.) As each wrong (worldly) view arises in the mind, we contemplate and deeply realize the corresponding transcendental truth that surfaces when we consider the basic facts of existence, as filled in the worksheet of example 2.

When we see things as they really are, that is against the backdrop of the basic facts of existence in this manner, we are able, with the power of the mind prepared by Samatha meditation, to intercept sensory impingements *before* information gets colored by wrong views. This is *bare attention -* that is, the bare object seen as it really is. Now we have the basis for seeing the object, or event with insight (wisdom). We have then realized what we earlier referred to as *experiential* knowledge, the step above intellectual knowledge.

To illustrate, recall the following 'slide show' steps (Chapter 7):
1. It is an object, white, moving.
2. It is a man.
3. It is Cousin Burl.
4. Cousin Burl is the selfish, mean and obnoxious person, who has never spoken a good word to me.

---

[31] Vipassana applies not only to situations of dukkha but also sukkha (happiness). However, states of happiness are transient and invariably return to dukkha.

[32] The reader may also want to try out example 1 for practice.

    5. I always end up in a confrontation with him.
    6. I hate Cousin Burl

As a base for seeing things as they really are (with the mind at 'neighborhood concentration'), our meditative grasp should be able to intercept the sensory data just after step 1 in this example. Then we have objectively seen form, color and movement only, and it is before the slightest subjective interpretation has arisen. Now we insightfully contemplate what is seen till the truths penetrate us in the light of the basic facts of existence.

As we begin to see Cousin Burl in the light of impermanence, egolessness and dukkha, our whole perspective and attitude change from negativity (illusion) to reality. Anger and aversion are replaced by compassion and unconditional love. The earlier biased view of Cousin Burl in isolation now changes to one that merges with a universal unbiased view applicable to all beings. Our own mental state presently changes from agitation to peace.

When the mind now moves to another object or event (a feeling, a sight, a noise etc.), we repeat the same process looking at it insightfully against the backdrop of impermanence, egolessnesss and dukkha. Then we move on either to the next object/event or 'home base' and so on into every aspect of daily living. Where worksheets have been filled and reviewed before this practice was begun, recall the thoughts recorded in them to facilitate contemplation, at the early stages of the practice.

As one progresses in the practice of Vipassana, applying it to everything that comes up in life, one's whole outlook on life, one's behavior and the manner of interaction with others and the world take on a totally different and increasingly wholesome flavor. The meditator's whole life begins to gradually move from dissatisfaction to joy. The culmination[33] of continued practice is the realization of a blissful state of mind hitherto not experienced, where everything without exception is seen exactly as they are, that is, in the light of impermanence and egolessness. The mind settles into a state of calmness and awareness where no fresh karma is produced. When there is no karma, there can be no birth; the cycle of birth and death comes to an end and the meditator realizes ultimate and permanent peace.

---

[33] This may happen in this lifetime or in a future life dependent on the refinement of one's practice and the dedication and effort the meditator puts into the practice. The reader interested in a detailed treatment of this phase of the practice should consult an acclaimed classic such as *The Heart of Buddhist Meditation* by Nyanaponika Thera and/or *The Path of Purification* by Bhikkhu Nanamoli and/or *Practical Insight Meditation* by Ven. Mahasi Sayadaw. They are published by the Buddhist Publication Society.

15

Conclusion

In this book we have covered some of the key principles of Buddhism and explored ways and means to apply them to our daily living. While the principles of Buddha's teachings are universal and timeless in their applicability, their actual application to an individual life has to become, in the final analysis, a personal endeavor. Buddha's Dhamma is an accurate road map[34] and we have to do the walking using it. The personal endeavor takes the form of diligent practice of the Dhamma. To quote Buddha's last words[35]; "*Strive with earnestness.*" In those three words lie the secret to the difference between continuing to suffer and eradication of suffering.

To strive with earnestness one needs a strong inner conviction that purification of one's own mind is the most important mission in his or her life from the present moment onwards. That conviction must be followed with persistent effort in the practice of Dhamma in daily life with a degree of determination reflected in the following words of Buddha[36]: "... I shall not give up my efforts till I have attained whatever is attainable by manly perseverance, energy and endeavor." Yet there must be the patience and understanding that the progress on the path will be gradual[37].

When a Buddhist is facing seemingly unsolvable adversity, it is not uncommon to hear him or her say: "If only Buddha was alive today, I would not be going through this." At times like these, one should recall Buddha's advice to his disciple Ananda just prior to his passing away: " For that which I have proclaimed and made known as the Dhamma and the Discipline, that shall be your Master when I am gone."

---

[34] "It is you who must make the effort. The Buddhas only show the way." From Dhammapada 276

[35] From the Maha Parinibbana Sutta

[36] Majjhima Nikaya, Sutta 70.

[37] "Bhikkhus, I do not say that final knowledge is achieved all at once. On the contrary, final knowledge is achieved by *gradual* training, by *gradual* practice, by *gradual* progress." Majjhima Nikaya, Sutta 70.

Buddha is not with us today, but the Dhamma is alive and well. So we need not use the fact of Buddha's absence as a self-fulfilling excuse to sink into hopelessness, whatever our adversity may be. In fact, in certain aspects, the Dhamma is doing much better today than it was in Buddha's time. During Buddha's lifetime one had to be in his presence (in India) to benefit from his wisdom, as there were no books on Dhamma at the time. Very few of the world's population were indeed fortunate to be able to listen to Buddha (and with the passage of time, his knowledgeable disciples). In contrast, today the Dhamma is, or can be made, easily accessible to any person anywhere in the world. So today's world is really better off than that of Buddha's era. All that is required of us today is a keenness to study and understand the principles of Dhamma and to practise diligently.

Furthermore, the struggle we face is small compared to Buddha's own thanks to Buddha himself. There was no Dhamma when he began the search - his monumental struggle to find the solution to suffering. There was no one to show him the way - no guiding light ahead of him. During his days of search he only knew what the problem was but not the solution, and groped in the dark until six years of search passed by. All he had was hope, determination, courage and absolute self-confidence that he will find the solution. Eventually he did find it - the unsurpassed Dhamma. Buddha had to *discover and apply*. We have only to *apply*.

Within the spectrum of Dhamma exists the means to transcend any human suffering, whether caused by a little irritant or the worst human tragedy. The Dhamma principles covered in this book should provide us with a solid basis from which to build the necessary individualized practice. With the right effort and discipline injected into that practice, we can gradually transcend dukkha and make constant progress towards inner peace, feeling the healing effects in our daily lives as we progress. Along the way, at some point, we will know we are at the start of the last lap. Then, with further help from Buddha's teachings, we will start to tread that last lap with confidence, and hopefully in this very life, reach the sublime state of ultimate peace.

When we realize the unsurpassed gift that Buddha left for us, we feel equally unsurpassed awe, respect and everlasting gratitude to him. The best that we can do to demonstrate that gratitude is to diligently practise Dhamma in our own lives and do all in our power to keep the Dhamma alive for the benefit of future generations. That would be the noblest mission we can ever hope to undertake in this life. So let us begin now and *strive with earnestness.*

Readers' Comments

The author welcomes comments from readers.
Please address c/o the publisher:

Kingsley Rajapakse
c/o Serena Publications
P.O. Box 29630
377 Burnhamthorpe Rd. East
Mississauga, Ontario
L5A 3Y1
Canada

ORDER FORM

Copies of *The Way to Inner Peace* can be ordered directly from the publisher by sending a *cheque or* money order (made payable to: *Serena Publications)* along with this form to:

> Serena Publications
> P. O. Box 29630
> 377 Burnhamthorpe Road East
> Mississauga, Ontario
> Canada L5A 3Y1

<u>Amount per book (within Canada)</u>

Book price	Cdn $8.95
Postage and handling	<u>1.85</u>
Sub-total	<u>*10.80*</u>
Add GST 7% (Canadian orders only)	<u>0.76</u>
Total	**$ 11.56**

<u>Postage and handling for orders from outside Canada</u>

U.S.A.	US $ 2.00
All other countries	US $ 4.00

(Please enter in BLOCK CAPITALS)

Your name: ....

Address: ....

....

....

....

Postal or ZIP code: ....

Phone Number: (*Area Code* ....) ....

Company or Business Name: ....